9/28/01
$12.95
B&T
As

# THE INFANTRY SOLDIER'S HANDBOOK

# Books by
# Major William H. Waldron

*Company Administration*

*Elements of Trench Warfare*

*The Infantry Soldier's Handbook*

*Scouting and Patrolling*

*Tactical Walks*

*What Sammy's Doing*

# The
# Infantry Soldier's
# Handbook

The Classic World War I Training Manual

By
MAJOR WILLIAM H. WALDRON
U.S. Infantry

THE LYONS PRESS

Printed in Canada

Originally published by The Harvey Press, 1917.

10   9   8   7   6   5   4   3   2   1

The Library of Congress Cataloging-in-Publication Data
is available on file.

# CONTENTS

# THE INFANTRY SOLDIER'S
# HANDBOOK

# CHAPTER I

## INFANTRY DRILL REGULATIONS

### DEFINITIONS

1. **BATTLE SIGHT.** The position of the rear sight when the leaf is laid down.

**COLUMN:** A formation in which the elements are placed one behind another. *For examples a column of files, single men placed behind each other; a column of squads, squads placed behind each other; column of companies, companies placed behind each other.*

**DEPLOY:** To extend the front. In general to change from column to line, or from close order to extended order. *For example, to deploy a squad means to place the men all on one line with greater intervals than they formerly had.*

**DISTANCE:** Space between elements in the direction of depth. Distance is measured from the back of the man in front to the breast of the man in rear. The distance between ranks is 40 inches in both line and column.

**FILE:** Two men, the front-rank man and the corresponding man of the rear rank. The front-rank man is the *file leader.* A file which has no rear-rank man is a *blank file.* The term *file* applies also to a single man in a single-rank formation.

**INTERVAL:** Space between elements of the same line. The interval between men in ranks is 4 inches and is measured from elbow to elbow. Between companies, squads, etc., it is measured from the left elbow of the left man or guide of the group on the right, to the right elbow of the right man or guide of the group on the left.

**LINE:** A formation in which the different elements are abreast of each other.

**ORDER, Close:** The formation in which the units, in double rank, are arranged in line or in column with normal intervals and distances.

**ORDER, Extended:** The formation in which the units are separated by intervals greater than in close order.

**PACE:** Thirty inches; the length of the full step in quick time.

**RANK:** A line of men placed side by side. *Troops are formed in double rank, that is two lines of men side by side.*

PART I—DRILL
**INTRODUCTION**

**2.** Success in battle is the ultimate object of all military training; success may be looked for only when the training is intelligent and thorough.

The excellence of an organization is judged by its field efficiency. The field efficiency of an organization depends primarily upon its effectiveness as a whole. Thoroughness and uniformity in the training of the units of an organization are indispensable to the efficiency of the whole; it is by such means alone that the requisite teamwork may be developed.

**3.** Simple movements and elastic formations are essential to correct training for battle.

**4.** The Drill Regulations are furnished as a guide. They provide the principles for training and for increasing the probability of success in battle.

In the interpretation of the regulations, the spirit must be sought. Quibbling over the minutiae of form is indicative of failure to grasp the spirit.

**5.** The following important distinctions must be observed:

(*a*) Drills executed at *attention* and the ceremonies are *disciplinary exercises* designed to teach precise and soldierly movement, and to inculcate that prompt and subconscious obedience which is essential to proper military control. To this end smartness and precision should be exacted in the execution of every detail. Such drills should be frequent, but short.

(*b*) The purpose of *extended order drill* is to teach the mechanism of deployment, of the firings, and, in general, of the employment of troops in combat. Such drills are in the nature of disciplinary exercises and should be frequent, thorough, and exact in order to habituate men to the firm control of their leaders. Extended order drill is executed *at ease*. The company is the largest unit which executes extended order drill.

(*c*) *Field exercises* are for instruction in the duties incident to campaign. Assumed situations are employed. Each exercise should conclude with a discussion, on the ground, of the exercise and principles involved.

(*d*) The *combat exercise, a form of field exercise* of the company, battalion, and larger units, consists of the *application of tactical principles* to assumed situations, employing in the execution the appropriate formations and movements of close and extended order.

Combat exercises must simulate, as far as possible, the battle conditions assumed. In order to familiarize both officers and men with such conditions, companies and battalions will frequently be consolidated to provide war-strength organizations. Officers and noncommissioned officers not required to complete the full quota of the units participating are assigned as observers or umpires.

The firing line can rarely be controlled by the voice alone; thorough training to insure the proper use of prescribed signals is necessary.

The exercise should be followed by a brief drill at attention in order to restore smartness and control.

**6.** In field exercises the enemy is said to be *imaginary* when his position and force are merely assumed; *outlined* when his position and force are indicated by a few men; *represented* when a body of troop acts as such.

## General Rules for Drills and Formations

**7.** When the *preparatory* command consists of more than one part, its elements are arranged as follows:

(1) For movements to be executed successively by the subdivisions or elements of an organization: (*a*) Description of the movement; (*b*) how executed, or on what element executed.

(2) For movements to be executed simultaneously by the subdivisions of an organization: (*a*) The designation of the subdivisions; (*b*) the movement to be executed.

**8.** Movements that may be executed toward either flank are explained as toward but one flank, it being necessary to substitute the word "left" for "right," and the reverse, to have the explanation of the corresponding movement toward the other flank. The commands are given for the execution of the movements toward either flank. The substitute word of the command is placed within parentheses.

**9.** Any movement may be executed either from the halt or when marching, unless otherwise prescribed. If at a halt, the command for movements involving maching need not be prefaced by *forward,* as 1. *Column right (left)*, 2. *MARCH.*

**10.** Any movement not specially excepted may be executed in double time.

If at a halt, or if marching in quick time, the command *double time* precedes the command of execution.

**11.** To hasten the execution of a movement begun in quick time, the command: 1. *Double time,* 2. *MARCH,* is given.

**12.** To stay the execution of a movement when marching, for the correction of errors, the command: 1. *In place,* 2. *HALT,* is given. All halt and stand fast, without changing the position of the pieces (Rifles).

To resume the movement the command: 1. *Resume,* 2. *MARCH,* is given.

**13.** To revoke a preparatory command, or, being at a halt, to begin anew a movement improperly begun, the command, *AS YOU WERE,* is given, at which the movement ceases and former position is resumed.

**14.** Unless otherwise announced, the guide of a company or subdivision of a company in line is *right;* of a battalion in line or line of subdivisions or of a deployed line, *center;* of a rank in column of squads, toward the side of the guide of the company.

To march with guide other than as prescribed above, or to change the guide: *Guide (right, left, or center).*

In successive formations into line, the guide is toward the point of rest; in platoons or larger subdivisions it is so announced.

The announcement of the guide, when given in connection with a movement, follows the command of execution for that movement. Exception: 1. *As skirmishers, guide right (left or center),* 2. *MARCH.* (*C. I. D. R., No.* 2.)

**15.** *The turn on the fixed pivot* by subdivisions is used in all formations from the line into column and the reverse.

*The turn on the moving pivot* is used by subdivisions of a column in executing changes of direction.

**16.** Partial changes of direction may be executed:

By interpolating in the preparatory command the word *half,* as *Column half right (left),* or *Right (left) half turn.* A change of direction of 45° is executed.

By the command: *INCLINE TO THE RIGHT (LEFT).* The guide or guiding element, moves in the indicated direction and the remainder of the command conforms. This movement effects slight changes of direction.

**17.** In close order, all details, detachments, and other bodies of troops are habitually formed in double rank.

To insure uniformity of interval between files when falling in, and in alignments, each man places the palm of the left hand upon the hip, fingers pointing downward. In the first case the hand is dropped by the side when the next man on the left has his interval; in the second case, at the command *front.*

## ORDERS, COMMANDS, AND SIGNALS

**18.** *Commands* only are employed in drill at attention. Otherwise either a *command, signal,* or *order* is employed, as best suits the occasion, or one may be used in conjunction with another.

**19.** Signals should be freely used in instruction, in order that officers and men may readily know them. In making arm signals the saber, rifle, or headdress may be held in the hand.

**20.** Officers and men fix their attention at the first word of command, the first note of the bugle or whistle, or the first motion of the signal. A signal includes both the preparatory command and the command of execution; the movement commences as soon as the signal is understood, unless otherwise prescribed.

**21.** Except in movements executed at *attention,* commanders or leaders of subdivisions repeat orders, commands, or signals whenever such repetition is deemed necessary to insure prompt and correct execution.

Officers, battalion noncommissioned staff officers, platoon leaders, guides, and musicians are equipped with whistles.

The major and his staff will use a whistle of distinctive tone; the captain and company musicians a second and distinctive whistle; the platoon leaders and guides a third distinctive whistle.

(*C. I. D. R., No.* 15.)

**22.** Prescribed signals are limited to such as are essential as a substitute for the voice under conditions which render the voice inadequate.

Before or during an engagement special signals may be agreed upon to facilitate the solution of such special difficulties as the particular situation is likely to develop, but it must be remembered that simplicity and certainty are indispensable qualities of a signal.

### Orders

**23.** In these regulations an *order* embraces instructions or directions given orally or in writing in terms suited to the particular occasion and not prescribed herein.

*Orders* are employed only when the *commands* prescribed herein do not sufficiently indicate the will of the commander.

### Commands

**24.** In these regulations a *command* is the will of the commander expressed in the phraseology prescribed herein.

**25.**—There are two kinds of commands:

The *preparatory* command, such as *forward,* indicates the movement that is to be executed.

The command of *execution,* such as *MARCH, HALT,* or *ARMS,* causes the execution.

*Preparatory* commands are distinguished by *italics,* those of *execution* by *CAPITALS.*

Where it is not mentioned in the text who gives the commands prescribed, they are to be given by the commander of the unit concerned.

The *preparatory* command should be given at such an interval of time before the command of *execution* as to admit of being properly understood; the command of *execution* should be given at the instant the movement is to commence.

The tone of command is animated, distinct, and of a loudness proportioned to the number of men for whom it is intended.

Each *preparatory* command is enunciated distinctly, with a rising inflection at the end, and in such manner that the command of *execution* may be more energetic.

The command of *execution* is firm in tone and brief.

**26.** Majors and commanders of units larger than a battalion repeat such commands of their superiors as are to be executed by their units, facing their units for that purpose. The battalion is the largest unit that executes a movement at the command of execution of its commander.

**27.** When giving commands to troops it is usually best to face toward them.

Indifference in giving commands must be avoided as it leads to laxity in execution. Commands should be given with spirit at all times.

### Bugle Signals

**28.** The following bugle signals may be used off the battle field, when not likely to convey information to the enemy:

*Attention*: Troops are brought to attention.

**ATTENTION**

**Attention to Orders: Troops fix their attention.**

ATTENTION TO ORDERS

**Forward, March:** Troops take up the march in quick time. This signal is also used to execute quick time from double time.

FORWARD, MARCH

**Double Time, March:** Troops take up the cadence of double time, 180 steps per minute, 36 inches to the step.

DOUBLE TIME, MARCH

**To the rear, March:** In close order troops execute. *Squads Right About.*

TO THE REAR, MARCH

**Halt.** Troops marching come to the halt.

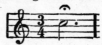

HALT

**Assemble, March:** Troops Assemble:

ASSEMBLY

The following bugle signals may be used on the battle field:

**Fix Bayonets:**

FIX BAYONETS

The major or senior officer in the firing line determines when bayonets shall be fixed and gives the proper command or signal. It is repeated by all parts of the firing line. Each man who was in the front rank prior to deployment, as soon as he recognizes the command or signal, suspends firing, quickly fixes his bayonet, and immediately resumes firing; after which the other men suspend firing, fix bayonets, and immediately resume firing. The support also fixes bayonets. The concerted fixing of the bayonet by the firing line at drill does not stimulate battle conditions and should not be required. It is essential that there be no marked pause in the firing. Bayonets will be fixed generally before or during the last, or second last, advance preceding the charge. (Par. 318.)

**Charge:**

CHARGE

Subject to orders from higher authority, the major determines the point from which the charge is to be made. The firing line having arrived at that point and being in readiness, the major causes the *charge* to be sounded. The signal is repeated by the musicians of all parts of the line. The company officers lead the charge. The skirmishers spring forward shouting, run with bayonets at charge, and close with the enemy. (Par. 319).

These signals are used only when intended for the entire firing line; hence they can be authorized only by the commander of a unit (for example, a regiment or brigade) which occupies a distinct section of the battle field. Exception: *Fix bayonet.*

The following bugle signals are used in exceptional cases on the battle field. Their principal uses are in field exercises and practice firing.

*Commence firing*: Officers charged with fire direction and control open fire as soon as practicable. When given to a firing line, the signal is equivalent to *fire at will.*

COMMENCE FIRING

*Cease firing*: All parts of the line execute *cease firing* at once.

These signals are not used by units smaller than a regiment, except when such unit is independent or detached from its regiment.

CEASE FIRING

## WHISTLE SIGNALS

**29.** *Attention to orders.* A *short blast* of the whistle. This signal is used on the march or in combat when necessary to fix the attention of troops, or of their commanders or leaders, preparatory to giving commands, orders, or signals.

When the firing line is firing, each squad leader suspends firing and fixes his attention at a *short blast* of his platoon leader's whistle. The platoon leader's subsequent commands or signals are repeated and enforced by the squad leader. If a squad leader's attention is attracted by a whistle other than that of his platoon leader, or if there are no orders or commands to convey to his squad he resumes firing at once.

*Suspend firing.* A *long blast* of the whistle.

All other whistle signals are prohibited.

(*C. I. D. R., No.* **15.**)

## ARM SIGNALS

30. The following arm signals are prescribed. In making signals either arm may be used. Officers who receive signals on the firing line "repeat back" at once to prevent misunderstanding.

Fig. 1

Forward

*FORWARD, MARCH.* Carry the hand to the shoulder; straighten and hold the arm horizontally, thrusting it in direction of march.

This signal is also used to execute quick time from double time.

*Signaled to the detached scout it is an order for him to move forward.*

*HALT.* Carry the hand to the shoulder; thrust the hand upward and hold the arm vertically.

*DOUBLE TIME, MARCH.* Carry the hand to the shoulder; rapidly thrust the hand upward the full extent of the arm several times.

Halt

Fig. 2

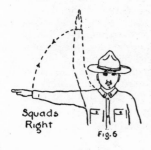

Squads Right

Fig. 6

*SQUADS RIGHT, MARCH.* Raise the arm laterally until horizontal; carry it to a vertical position above the head and swing it several times between the vertical and horizontal positions.

*Signaled to the detached scout it is an order to move by the right flank until signaled to go forward, to the rear, or halt.*

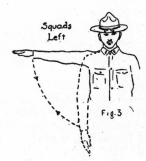

*SQUADS LEFT, MARCH.* Raise the arm laterally until horizontal; carry it downward to the side and swing it several times between the downward and horizontal positions.

*Signaled to the detached scout move to the left flank until signaled to go forward, to the rear or halt.*

*SQUADS RIGHT ABOUT, MARCH* (if in close order) or, *TO THE REAR, MARCH* (if in skirmish line) extend the arm vertically above the head; carry it laterally downward to the side and swing it several times between the vertical and downward positions.

*Signaled to the detached scout to move to the rear until another signal is given.*

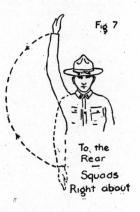

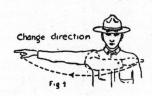

*CHANGE DIRECTION OF COLUMN, RIGHT (L E F T), MARCH.* The hand on the side toward which the change of direction is to be made is carried across the body to the opposite shoulder, forearm horizontal; then swing in a horizontal plane, arm extended, pointing in the new direction.

Fig 5

As Skirmishers

*AS SKIRMISHERS, MARCH.* Raise both arms laterally until horizontal.

Signaled to the detached scout or by the detached scout to the patrol leader this signal means, "Have important information." In which case one of the spare men is sent to relieve the scout in order that he may come in with his information, or the patrol leader joins him. (See Scouting and Patrolling for full details of communication between members of a patrol).

*AS SKIRMISHERS, GUIDE CENTER MARCH.* Raise both arms laterally until horizontal; swing both simultaneously upward until vertical and return to the horizontal; repeat several times.

Skirmishers Guide Center    Fig. 8

*AS SKIRMISHERS, GUIDE RIGHT (LEFT), MARCH.* Raise both arms laterally until horizontal; hold the arm on the side of the guide steadily in the horizontal position; swing the other upward until vertical and return it to the horizontal; repeat several times.

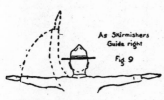

As Skirmishers Guide right

Fig 9

*ASSEMBLE, MARCH.* Raise the arm vertically to its full extent and describe horizontal circles.

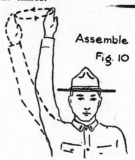

Assemble

Fig. 10

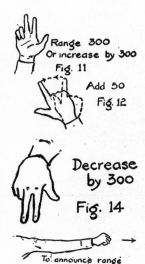

Range 300
Or increase by 300
Fig. 11

Add 50
Fig. 12

Decrease
by 300
Fig. 14

To announce range
Battle sight
Fig. 13

*Range,* or *Change elevation.* To announce *range,* extend the arm toward the leaders or men for whom the signal is intended, fist closed; by keeping the fist closed battle sight is indicated; by opening and closing the fist, expose thumb and fingers to a number equal to the hundreds of yards; to add 50 yards describe a short horizontal line with forefinger. *To change elevation;* indicate the *amount of increase* or *decrease* by fingers as above; point upward to indicate increase and downward to indicate decrease.

*What range are you using?* or *What is the range?* Extend the arms toward the person addressed, one hand open, palm to the front, resting on the other hand, fist closed.

What range are you using
or What is the
range?          Fig 19

Fig. 20

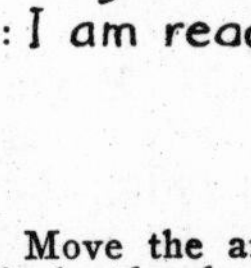

Are you ready?
or *I am ready.*
Raise the hand, fingers extended and joined, palm toward the person addressed.

Are you ready
or: I am ready

Fig 18
Commence Firing

*Commence firing.* Move the arm extended in full length, hand palm down, several times through a horizontal arc in front of the body.
*Fire faster.* Execute rapidly the signal "Commence firing."
*Fire slower.* Execute slowly the signal "Commence firing."

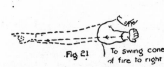

.Fig 21 To swing cone of fire to right

*To swing the cone of fire to the right, or left.* Extend the arm in full length to the front, palm to the right (left); swing the arm to right (left), and point in the direction of the new target.

*Fix bayonet.* Simulate the movement of the right hand in "Fix bayonet."

(Simulate: Grasp the handle of the bayonet with the right hand, back of hand towards the body; (simulate) drawing of bayonet from the scabbard and placing it on the rifle.)

*Suspend firing.* Raise and hold the forearm steadily in a horizontal position in front of the forehead, palm of the hand to the front.

*Cease firing.* Raise the forearm as in *suspend firing* and swing it up and down several times in front of the face.

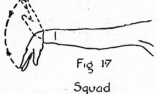

Suspend firing
For Cease firing - Swing arm up and down several times
Fig. 15.

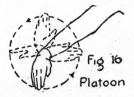

Fig 16
Platoon

*Platoon.* Extend the arm horizontally toward the platoon leader; swing the hand up and down from the wrist.

*Squad.* Extend the arm horizontally toward the platoon leader; swing the hand up and down from the wrist.

Fig 17
Squad

*Rush.* Same as *double time.* (*C. I. D. R., Nos. 2 and* 14.)

The signals *platoon* and *squad* are intended primarily for communication between the captain and his platoon leaders. The signal *platoon* or *squad* indicates that the platoon commander is to cause the signal which follows to be executed by platoon or squad.

## Flag Signals

**31** The signal flags described below are carried by the company musicians in the field.

In a regiment in which it is impracticable to make the permanent battalion division alphabetically, the flags of a battalion are as shown; flags are assigned to the companies alphabetically, within their respective battalions, in the order given below.

First battalion:

Company A. Red field, white square.

Company B. Red field, blue square.

Company C. Red field, white diagonals.

Company D. Red field, blue diagonals.

Second battalion:

Company E. White field, red square.

Company F. White field, blue square.

Company G. White field, red diagonals.

Company H. White field, blue diagonals.

Third battalion:

Company I. Blue field, red square.

Company K. Blue field, white square.

Company L. Blue field, red diagonals.

Company M. Blue field, white diagonals.

**32.** In addition to their use in visual signaling, these flags serve to mark the assembly point of the company when disorganized by combat, and to mark the location of the company in bivouac and elsewhere, when such use is desirable.

**33.** (1) For communication between the firing line and the reserve or commander in the rear, the subjoined signals (Signal Corps codes) are prescribed and should be memorized. In transmission, their concealment from the enemy's view should be insured. In the absence of signal flags, the head-dress or other substitute may be used.

| Letter of alphabet. | If signaled from the rear to the firing line. | If signaled from the firing line to the rear. |
|---|---|---|
| A M ........ | Ammunition going forward | Ammunition required. |
| C C C ....... | Charge (mandatory at all times) | Am about to charge if no in-structions to the contrary. |
| C F .......... | Cease firing .............. | Cease firing. |
| D T .......... | Double time or "rush" .... | Double time or "rush." |
| F ............. | Commence firing .......... | Commence firing. |
| F B .......... | Fix Bayonets ............. | Fix bayonets. |
| F L ......... | Artillery fire is causing us losses. | Artillery fire is causing us losses. |
| G ........... | Move forward ............. | Preparing to move forward. |
| H H H ...... | Halt ..................... | Halt. |
| K ............ | Negative ................. | Negative. |
| L T ......... | Left ..................... | Left. |
| O ........... (A r d o i s and s e m a p h o r e only.) | What is the (R. N. etc.)? Interrogatory. | What is the (R N. etc.)? Interrogatory. |
| - - — — - - (All methods but ardois and semaphore.) | What is the (R. N. etc.)? Interrogatory. | What is the (R. N. etc.)? Interrogatory. |
| P ............ | Affirmative ............. | Affirmative. |
| R ............ | Acknowledgment ......... | Acknowledgment. |
| R N ......... | Range ................. | Range. |
| R T ......... | Right ................... | Right. |
| S S S ........ | Support going forward .... | Support needed. |
| S U F ...... | Suspend firing ............ | Suspend firing. |
| T ........... | Target .................. | Target. |

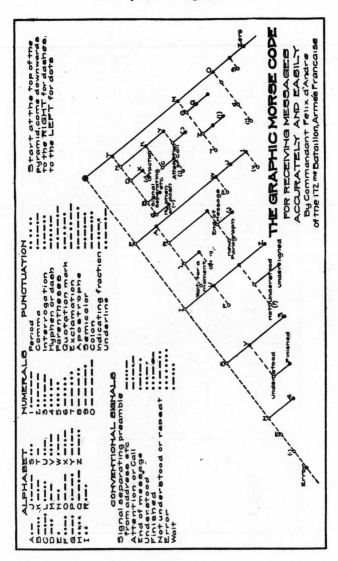

THE GRAPHIC MORSE CODE

FOR RECEIVING MESSAGES
ACCURATELY AND EASILY
By Commandant Felix d'Andre
of the 172 me Bataillon, Armée Francaise

## TWO-ARM SEMAPHORE CODE.

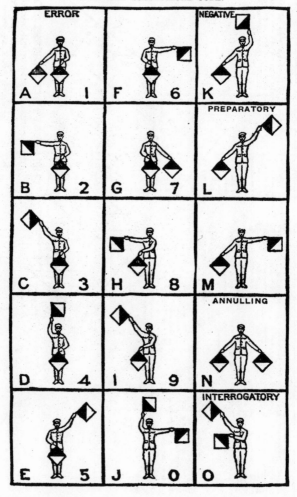

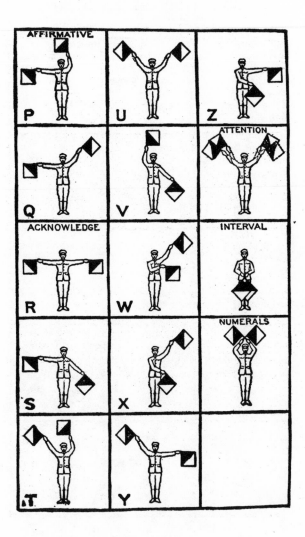

## SCHOOL OF THE SOLDIER

**34.** The instructor explains briefly each movement, first executing it himself if practicable. He requires the recruits to take the proper positions unassisted and does not touch them for the purpose of correcting them, except when they are unable to correct themselves. He avoids keeping them too long at the same movement, although each should be understood before passing to another. He exacts by degrees the desired precision and uniformity.

**35.** In order that all may advance as rapidly as their abilities permit, the recruits are grouped according to proficiency as instruction progresses. Those who lack aptitude and quickness are separated from the others and placed under experienced drill masters.

## INSTRUCTION WITHOUT ARMS

**36.** For preliminary instruction a number of recruits, usually not exceeding three or four, are formed as a squad in single rank.

### The Rests

**37.** Being at a halt, the commands are: *FALL OUT; REST; AT EASE;* and, 1. *Parade,* 2. *Rest.*

At the command *fall out,* the men may leave the ranks, but are required to remain in the immediate vicinity. They resume their former places, at attention, at the command *fall in.*

At the command *rest* each man keeps one foot in place, but is not required to preserve silence or immobility.

**38.**

Head erect and squarely to the front.
Eyes straight to the front.
Chin drawn in so that axis of head and neck is vertical.
Shoulders square and falling equally.
Chest lifted and arched.

Arms and hands hanging naturally.
Hips level and drawn back slightly.
Body erect and resting equally on hips.
Thumbs along the seam of the trousers.

Knees straight without stiffness.
Heels on the same line and as near each other as the conformation of the man permits.
Feet turned out equally and forming an angle of 45°.
Weight of body resting equally on the heels and balls of the feet.

THE POSITION OF THE SOLDIER, OR "ATTENTION".

**39.** 1. *Parade,* 2. *REST.* Carry the right foot 6 inches straight to the rear, left knee slightly bent; clasp the hands, without constraint, in front of the center of the body, fingers joined, left hand uppermost, left thumb clasped by the thumb and forefinger of the right hand; preserve silence and steadiness of position.

> *The soldier stands at Parade Rest, when in formation, not under arms at "Retreat", while the Field music sounds the call.*
>
> *(For Parade Rest under Arms, see paragraph 84).*
>
> *Cautions:*
>
> *Do not lean the body forward or back.*
>
> *Do not place the right hand on top.*
>
> *Do not bend the right knee.*
>
> *Do not have the fingers of the left hand spread apart.*
>
> *Move the right foot straight to the rear, not to the right rear.*

PARADE REST

**40.** To resume the attention: 1. *Squad,* 2. *ATTENTION.* The men take the position of the soldier.

### Eyes Right or Left.

**41.** 1. *Eyes,* 2. *RIGHT (LEFT),* 3. *FRONT.*

At the command *right,* turn the head to the right oblique, eyes fixed on the line of eyes of the men in, or supposed to be in, the same rank. At the command *front,* turn the head and eyes to the front.

*Eyes Right is used in dressing a line and to render the salute to the reviewing officer when troops are passing in review during ceremonies. Cautions:*

*Do not turn the body, keep it square to the front.*

*Do not draw the chin down.*

EYES RIGHT

### Facings.

**42.** To the flank: 1. *Right (left)*, 2. *FACE.*

Raise slightly the left heel and right toe; face to the right, turning on the right heel, assisted by a slight pressure on the ball of the left foot; place the left foot by the side of the right. Left face is executed on the left heel in the corresponding manner.

*Right (left) half face* is executed similarly, facing 45°.

"To face in marching" and advance, turn on the ball of either foot and step off with the other foot in the new line of direction; to face in marching without gaining ground in the new direction, turn on the ball of either foot and mark time.

**43.** To the rear: 1. *About*, 2. *FACE.*

**RIGHT FACE**

Carry the toe of the right foot about a half foot-length to the rear and slightly to the left of the left heel without changing the position of the left foot; face to the rear, turning to the right on the left heel and right toe; place the right heel by the side of the left.

**HAND SALUTE**

### Salute with the Hand

**44.** 1. *Hand*, 2. *SALUTE.*

Raise the right hand smartly till the tip of the forefinger touches the lower part of the headdress or forehead above the right eye, thumb and fingers extended and joined, palm to the left, forearm inclined at about 45°, hand and wrist straight; at the same time look toward the person saluted. (*TWO*) Drop the arm smartly by the side.

**HAND SALUTE**
**(PROFILE)**

## HONORS AND SALUTES

**45.** (1) Salutes shall be exchanged between officers and enlisted men not in a military formation, nor at drill, work, games, or mess, on every occasion of their meeting, passing near or being addressed, the officer junior in rank or enlisted man saluting first.

(2) When an officer enters a room where there are several enlisted men, the word "attention" is given by some one who perceives him, when all rise, uncover, and remain standing at attention until the officer leaves the room or directs otherwise. Enlisted men at meals stop eating and remain seated at attention.

(3) An enlisted man, if seated, rises on the approach of an officer, faces toward him, stands at attention and salutes. Standing he faces an officer for the same purpose. If the parties remain in the same place or on the same ground, such compliments need not be repeated. Soldiers actually at work do not cease work to salute an officer unless addressed by him.

(4) Before addressing an officer, an enlisted man makes the prescribed salute with the weapon with which he is armed, or, if unarmed, with the right hand. He also makes the same salute after receiving a reply.

(5) In uniform, covered or uncovered, but not in formation, officers and enlisted men salute military persons as follows: With arms in hand, the salute prescribed for that arm (sentinels on interior guard duty excepted) ; without arms, the right-hand salute.

(6) In civilian dress, covered or uncovered, officers and enlisted men salute military persons with the right-hand salute.

(7) Officers and enlisted men will render the prescribed salutes in a military manner, the officer junior in rank, or the enlisted men, saluting first. When several officers in company are saluted, all entitled to the salute shall return it.

(8) Except in the field under campaign or simulated campaign conditions, a mounted officer (or soldier) dismounts before addressing a superior officer not mounted.

(9) A man in formation shall not salute when directly addressed, but shall come to attention if at rest or at ease.

(10) Saluting distance is that within which recognition is easy. In general, it does not exceed 30 paces.

(11) When an officer entitled to the salute passes in rear of a body of troops, it is brought to attention while he is opposite the post of the commander.

(12) In public conveyances, such as railway trains and street cars, and in public places, such as theaters, honors and personal salutes may be omitted when palpably inappropriate or apt to disturb or annoy civilians present.        '

(13) Soldiers at all times and in all situations pay the same compliments to officers of the Army, Navy, Marine Corps, and Volunteers, and to officers of the National Guard as to officers of their own regiment, corps, or arm of service.

(14) Sentinels on post doing interior guard duty conform to the foregoing principles, but salute by presenting arms when armed with the rifle. They will not salute if it interferes with the proper performance of their duties. Troops under arms will salute as prescribed in drill regulations. (1. D. R. 759).

**46.** (1) Commanders of detachments or other commands will salute officers of grades higher than the person commanding the unit, by first bringing the unit to attention and then saluting as required by subparagraph (5), paragraph 759 If the person saluted is of a junior or equal grade, the unit need not be at attention in the exchange of salutes.

(2) If two detachments or other commands meet, their commanders will exchange salutes, both commands being at attention. (I. D. R. 760).

**47.** Salutes and honors, as a rule, are not paid by troops actually engaged in drill, on the march, or in the field under campaign or simulated campaign conditions. Troops on the service of security pay no compliments whatever. (I. D. R. 761).

**48.** If the command is in line at a halt (not in the field) and armed with the rifle, or with sabers drawn, it shall be brought to *present arms* or *present sabers* before its commander salutes in the following cases: When the National Anthem is played, or when *to the color* or *to the standard* is sounded during ceremonies, or when a person is saluted who is its immediate or higher commander or a general officer, or when the national or regimental color is saluted. (I. D. R. 762).

**49.** At parades and other ceremonies, under arms, the command shall render the prescribed salute and shall remain in the position of salute while the National Anthem is being played; also at retreat and during ceremonies when *to the color* is played, if no band is present. If not under arms, the organizations shall be brought to attention at the first note of the National Anthem, *to the color* or *to the standard,* and the salute rendered by the officer or noncommissioned officer in command as prescribed in regulations, as amended herein. (I. D. R. 763).

**50.** Whenever the National Anthem is played at any place when persons belonging to the military service are present, all officers and enlisted men not in formation shall stand at attention facing toward the music (except at retreat, when they shall face toward the flag). If in uniform, covered or uncovered, or in civilian clothes, uncovered, they shall salute at the first note of the anthem, retaining the position of salute until the last note of the anthem. If not in uniform and covered, they shall uncover at the first note of the anthem, holding the headdress opposite the left shoulder and so remain until its close, except that in inclement weather the headdress may be slightly raised.

The same rules apply when *to the color* or *to the standard* is sounded as when the National Anthem is played.

When played by an Army band, the National Anthem shall be played through without repetition of any part not required to be repeated to make it complete.

The same marks of respect prescribed for observance during the playing of the National Anthem of the United States shall be shown toward the national anthem of any other country when played upon official occasions. (I. D. R. 764).

**51.** Officers and enlisted men passing the uncased color will render honors as follows: If in uniform, they will salute as required by subparagraph (5), paragraph 759; if in civilian dress and covered, they will uncover, holding the headdress opposite the left shoulder with the right hand; if uncovered they will salute with the right-hand salute. (I. D. R. 765).

## STEPS AND MARCHINGS

**52.** All steps and marchings executed from a halt, except right step, begin with the left foot.

**53.** The length of the full step in quick time is 30 inches, measured from heel to heel, and the cadence is at the rate of 120 steps per minute.

The length of the full step in double time is 36 inches; the cadence is at the rate of 180 steps per minute.

The instructor, when necessary, indicates the cadence of the step by calling *one, two, three, four,* or *left, right,* the instant the left and right foot, respectively, should be planted.

**54.** All steps and marchings and movements involving march are executed in *quick time* unless the squad be marching in *double time,* or *double time* be added to the command; in the latter case *double time* is added to the preparatory command. Example: 1. *Squad right, double time,* 2. *MARCH* (School of the Squad).

FORWARD, MARCH

### Quick Time

**55.** Being at a halt, to march forward in quick time; 1. *Forward,* 2. *MARCH.*

At the command *forward,* shift the weight of the body to the right leg, left knee straight.

At the command *march,* move the left foot smartly straight forward 30 inches from the right, sole near the ground, and plant it without shock; next, in like manner, advance the right foot and plant it as above; continue the march. The arms swing naturally.

*Caution:*

*Do not move the body perceptibly when you shift the weight to the right leg.*

*Take the full 30-inch step on the "step off." Don't "crow-hop."*

DOUBLE TIME

**56.** Being at a halt, or in march in quick time, to march in double time: 1. *Double time,* 2. *MARCH.*

If at a halt, at the first command shift the weight of the body to the right leg. At the command *march,* raise the forearms, fingers closed, to a horizontal position along the waist line; take up an easy run with the step and cadence of double time, allowing a natural swinging motion to the arms.

If marching in quick time, at the command *march,* given as either foot strikes the ground, take one step in quick time, and then step off in double time.

**57.** To resume the quick time: 1. *Quick time,* 2. *MARCH.*

At the command *march,* given as either foot strikes the ground, advance and plant the other foot in double time; resume the quick time, dropping the hands by the sides.

## To Mark Time

.**58.** Being in march: 1. *Mark time,* 2. *MARCH.*

At the command *march,* given as either foot strikes the ground, advance and plant the other foot; bring up the foot in rear and continue the cadence by alternately raising each foot about 2 inches and planting it on line with the other.

Being at a halt, at the command *march,* raise and plant the feet as described above.

## The Half Step

**59.** 1. *Half step,* 2. *MARCH.*

Take steps of 15 inches in quick time, 18 inches in double time.

**60.** *Forward, half step, halt,* and *mark time* may be executed one from the other in quick or double time.

To resume the full step from half step or mark time: 1. *Forward,* 2. *MARCH.*

### Side Step

**61.** Being at a halt or mark time: 1. *Right (left) step,* 2. *MARCH.*

Carry and plant the right foot 15 inches to the right; bring the left foot beside it and continue the movement in the cadence of quick time.

The side step is used for short distances only and is not executed in double time.

If at order arms, the side step is executed *at trail* without command.

### Back Step

**62.** Being at a halt or mark time: 1. *Backward,* 2. *MARCH.*

RIGHT STEP

Take steps of 15 inches straight to the rear.

The back step is used for short distances only and is not executed in double time.

If at order arms, the back step is executed *at trail* without command.

### To Halt

**63.** To arrest the march in quick or double time: 1. *Squad,* 2. *HALT.*

At the command *halt,* given as either foot strikes the ground, plant the other foot as in marching; raise and place the first foot by the side of the other. If in double time, drop the hands by the sides.

### To March by the Flank

**64.** Being in march: 1. *By the right (left) flank,* 2. *MARCH.*

At the command *march,* given as the right foot strikes the ground, advance and plant the left foot, then face to the right in marching and step off in the new direction with the right foot.

## To March to the Rear

**65.** Being in march: 1. *To the rear,* 2. *MARCH.*

At the command *march,* given as the right foot strikes the ground, advance and plant the left foot; turn to the right about on the balls of both feet and immediately step off with the left foot.

If marching in double time, turn to the right about, taking four steps in place, keeping the cadence, and then step off with the left foot.

## Change Step

**66.** . Being in march: 1. *Change step,* 2. *MARCH.*

At the command *march,* given as the right foot strikes the ground, advance and plant the left foot; plant the toe of the right foot near the heel of the left and step off with the left foot.

The change on the right foot is similarly executed, the command *march* being given as the left foot strikes the ground.

At the command *at ease* each man keeps one foot in place and is required to preserve silence but not immobility.

## Manual of Arms

**67.** As soon as practicable the recruit is taught the use, nomenclature (Pl. I), and care of his rifle; when fair progress has been made in the instruction without arms, he is taught the manual of arms; instruction without arms and that with arms alternate.

**68.** The following rules govern the carrying of the piece:

**First.** The piece is not carried with cartridges in either the chamber or the magazine, except when specifically ordered. When so loaded, or supposed to be loaded, it is habitually carried locked; that is, with the *safety lock* turned to the "safe." At all other times it is carried unlocked, with the trigger pulled.

Second. Whenever troops are formed under arms, pieces are immediately inspected at the commands: 1. *Inspection,* 2. *ARMS;* 3. *Order* (*Right shoulder, port*), 4. *ARMS.*

A similar inspection is made immediately before dismissal.

If cartridges are found in the chamber of magazine they are removed and placed in the belt.

Third. The cut-off is kept turned "off" except when cartridges are actually used.

Fourth. The bayonet is not fixed except in bayonet exercise, on guard, or for combat.

Fifth. *Fall in* is executed with the piece at the order arms *Fall out, rest,* and *at ease* are executed as without arms. On resuming *attention* the position of order arms is taken.

Sixth. If at the order, unless otherwise prescribed, the piece is brought to the right shoulder at the command *march,* the three motions corresponding with the first three steps. Movements may be executed at the trail by prefacing the preparatory command with the words *at trail;* as, 1. *At trail, forward.* 2. *MARCH;* the trail is taken at the command *march.*

When the facings, alignments, open and close ranks, taking interval or distance, and assemblings are executed from the order, raise the piece to the trail while in motion and resume the order on halting.

Seventh. The piece is brought to the order on halting. The execution of the order begins when the halt is completed.

Eighth. A disengaged hand in double time is held as when without arms.

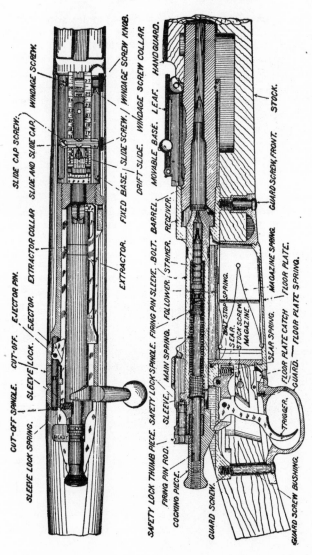

PLATE I

**70.** The following rules govern the execution of the manual of arms:

First. In all positions of the left hand at the balance (center of gravity, bayonet unfixed) the thumb clasps the piece; the sling is included in the grasp of the hand.

Second. In all positions of the piece "diagonally across the body" the position of the piece, left arm and hand are the same as in port arms.

Third. In resuming the order from any position in the manual, the motion next to the last concludes with the butt of the piece about 3 inches from the ground, barrel· to the rear, the left hand above and near the right, steadying the piece, fingers extended and joined, forearm and wrist straight and inclining downward, all fingers of the right hand grasping the piece. To complete the order, lower the piece gently to the ground with the right hand, drop the left quickly by the side, and take the position of order arms.

Allowing the piece to drop through the right hand to the ground, or other similar abuse of the rifle to produce effect in executing the manual, is prohibited.

Fourth. The cadence of the motions is that of quick time; the recruits are first required to give their whole attention to the details of the motions, the cadence being gradually acquired as they become accustomed to handling their pieces. The instructor may require them to count aloud in cadence with the motions.

Fifth. The manual is taught at a halt and the movements are, for the purpose of instruction, divided into motions and executed in detail; in this case the command of *execution* determines the prompt execution of the first motion, and the commands, *two, three, four,* that of the other motions.

To execute the movements in detail, the instructor first cautions: *By the numbers;* all movements divided into motions are then executed as above explained until he cautions: *Without the numbers;* or commands movements other than those in the manual of arms.

Sixth. Whenever circumstances require, the regular positions of the manual of arms and the firings may be ordered without regard to the previous position of the piece.

Under exceptional conditions of weather or fatigue the rifle may be carried in any manner directed.

71. *Position of order arms standing*: The butt rests evenly on the ground, barrel to the rear, toe of the butt on a line with toe of, and touching, the right shoe, arms and hands hanging naturally, right hand holding the piece between the thumb and fingers.

ORDER ARMS

ORDER ARMS

72. Being at order arms: 1. *Present, 2. ARMS.*

With the right hand carry the piece in front of the center of the body, barrel to the rear and vertical, grasp it with the left hand at the balance, forearm horizontal and resting against the body (*TWO*) Grasp the small of the stock with the right hand.

*Cautions:*

*Do not incline the muzzle of the piece to the front or rear. Hold it vertical.*

*When the piece is raised with the right hand, be careful to see that it is not raised too high. If it is an extra movement is necessary to bring it into the proper position.*

PRESENT ARMS
(1)

PRESENT ARMS
(2)

**73.** Being at order arms: 1. *Port*, 2. *ARMS*.

With the right hand raise and throw the piece diagonally across the body, grasp it smartly with both hands; the right, palm down, at the small of the stock; the left, palm up, at the balance; barrel up, sloping to the left and crossing opposite the junction of the neck with the left shoulder; right forearm horizontal; left forearm resting against the body; the piece in a vertical plane parallel to the front.

*Cautions:*
*Do not have the barrel sloping too far to the left.*
*In throwing the piece up to the position, do not move the body to the right or left.*

**74.** Being at present arms: 1. *Port*, 2. *ARMS*.
Carry the piece to a vertical position in front take the position of port arms.

**75.** Being at port arms: 1. *Present*, 2. *ARMS*.
Carry the piece diagonally across the body and

PORT ARMS

of the center of the body and take the position of present arms.

**76.** Being at present or port arms: 1. *Order*, 2. *ARMS*.

Let go with the right hand; lower and carry the piece to the right with the left hand; re-grasp it with the right hand just above the lower band; let go with the left hand, and take the next to the last position in coming to the order. (*TWO*) Complete the order.

**77.** In resuming the order from any position in the manual, the motion next to the last concludes with the butt of the piece about 3 inches from the ground, barrel to the rear, the left hand above and near the right, steadying the piece, fingers extended and joined, forearm and wrist straight and inclining downward, all fingers of the right hand grasping the piece. To complete the order, lower the piece gently to the ground with the right hand, drop the left quickly by the side, and take the position of order arms.

Allowing the piece to drop through the right hand to the ground, or other similar abuse of the rifle to produce effect in executing the manual, is prohibited.

NEXT TO LAST
POSITION OF
ORDER ARMS

ORDER ARMS          ONE          TWO          THREE

RIGHT SHOULDER ARMS

**78.** Being at order arms: 1. *Right shoulder,* 2. *ARMS.*

With the right hand raise and throw the piece diagonally across the body; carry the right hand quickly to the butt, embracing it, the heel between the first two fingers. (*TWO*) Without changing the grasp of the right hand, place the piece on the right shoulder, barrel up and inclined at an angle of about 45° from the horizontal, trigger guard in the hollow of the shoulder, right elbow near the side, the piece in a vertical plane perpendicular to the front; carry the left hand, thumb and fingers extended and joined, to the small of the stock, tip of the forefinger touching the cocking piece, wrist straight and elbow down. (*THREE*) Drop the left hand by the side. *Cautions:*

1. *Do not duck the head to the left when the piece is placed on the shoulder.*

2. *Do not move the body when bringing the piece up to the first position.*

3. *Do not rest the trigger guard on top of the shoulder.*

4. *Hold the right firearm horizontal, any other position deranges the position of the piece materially.*

**79.** Being at right shoulder arms: 1. *Order,* 2. *ARMS.*

Press the butt down quickly and throw the piece diagonally across the body, the right hand retaining the grasp of the butt. *(TWO), (THREE)* Execute order arms as described from port arms.

*Cautions:*

1. *Do not duck the head to the left when the piece is removed from the shoulder.*

2. *Do not throw the piece too far to the front when it is brought down to the first position.*

**80.** Being at port arms: 1. *Right shoulder,* 2. *ARMS.*

Change the right hand to the butt. *(TWO), (THREE)* As in right shoulder arms from order arms.

**80a.** Being at right shoulder arms: 1. *Port,* 2. *ARMS.*

Press the butt down quickly and throw the piece diagonally across the body, the right hand retaining its grasp of the butt. *(TWO)* Change the right hand to the small of the stock.

**81.** Being at right shoulder arms: 1. *Present,* 2. *ARMS.*

Execute port arms. *(THREE)* Execute present arms.

**82.** Being at present arms: 1. *Right shoulder,* 2. *ARMS.*

Execute port arms *(TWO), (THREE), (FOUR)* Execute right shoulder arms as from port arms.

*Cautions:*

1. *Make each movement distinct in itself. Do not slight any of them.*

2. *At (Two) let go of the small of the stock with the right hand and grasp the butt of the piece as in coming to the first position of the right shoulder from the order.*

**83.** Being at port arms: 1. *Left shoulder,* 2. *ARMS.*

Carry the piece with the right hand and place it on the left shoulder, barrel up, trigger guard in the hollow of the shoulder; at the same time grasp the butt with the left hand, heel between first and second fingers, thumb and fingers closed on the stock. *(TWO)* Drop the right hand by the side.

Being at left shoulder arms: 1. *Port,* 2. *ARMS.*

Grasp the piece with the right hand at the small of the stock. *(TWO)* Carry the piece to the right with the right hand, regrasp it with the left, and take the position of port arms.

*Left shoulder arms* may be ordered directly from the order, right shoulder or present, or the reverse. At the command arms execute *port arms* and continue in cadence to the position ordered.

**84.** Being at order arms: 1. *Parade*, 2. *REST*.

Carry the right foot 6 inches straight to the rear, left knee slightly bent; carry the muzzle in front of the center of the body, barrel to the left; grasp the piece with the left hand just below the stacking swivel, and with the right hand below and against the left.

Being at parade rest: 1. *Squad*, 2. *ATTENTION*.

Resume the order, the left hand quitting the piece opposite the right hip.

*The position of "Parade Rest" is used:*

*1. At Retreat formation, under Arms, while the Field music sounds the call.*

*2. At Parades and Guard Mount while the band is "Trooping the Line."*

*3. At funerals, during the ceremonies at the grave of the deceased.*

**PARADE REST**

**85.** Being at order arms: 1. *Trail*, 2. *ARMS.*

Raise the piece, right arm slightly bent, and incline the muzzle forward so that the barrel makes an angle of about 30° with the vertical.

When it can be done without danger or inconvenience to others, the piece may be grasped at the balance and the muzzle lowered until the piece is horizontal; a similar position in the left hand may be used.

**86.** Being at trail arms: 1. *Order*, 2. *ARMS.*

Lower the piece with the right hand and resume the order.

*The Position of Trail Arms is used:*

*1. Dressing the element.*

*2. When Ranks are opened.*

*3. When individuals move in a formation to rectify their position.*

*4. Taking intervals and distances.*

*5. Right and left step.*

*6. When deployed as skirmishers.*

**TRAIL ARMS**

## THE RIFLE SALUTE

**87.** Being at right shoulder arms: 1. *Rifle,* 2. *SALUTE.*

Carry the left hand smarly to the small of the stock, forearm horizontal, palm of hand down, thumb and fingers extended and joined, forefinger touching end of cocking piece; look toward the person saluted. (*TWO*) Drop left hand by the side; turn head and eyes to the front.

**88.** Being at order or trail arms: 1. *Rifle,* 2. *SALUTE.*

Carry the left hand smartly to the right side, palm of the hand down, thumb and fingers extended and joined, forefinger against piece near the muzzle; look toward the person saluted.

(*TWO*) Drop the left hand by the side; turn the head and eyes to the front.

For rules governing salutes see "Honors and Salutes," pars. 45 to 51 ante.

## The Bayonet

**89.** Being at order arms: 1. *Fix,* 2. *BAYONET.*

If the bayonet scabbard is carried on the belt: Execute parade rest; grasp the bayonet with the right hand, back of hand toward the body; draw the bayonet from the scabbard and fix it on the barrel, glancing at the muzzle; resume the order.

If the bayonet is carried on the haversack: Draw the bayonet with the left hand and fix it in the most convenient manner.

**90.** Being at order arms: 1. *Unfix,* 2. *BAYONET.*

If the bayonet scabbard is carried on the belt: Execute parade rest; grasp the handle of the bayonet firmly with the right hand, pressing the spring with the forefinger of the right hand; raise the bayonet until the handle is about 12 inches above the muzzle of the piece; drop the point to the left, back of the hand toward the body, and, glancing at the scabbard, return the bayonet, the blade passing between the left arm and the body; regrasp the piece with the right hand and resume the order.

FIX BAYONET            UNFIX BAYONET

If the bayonet scabbard is carried on the haversack: Take the bayonet from the rifle with the left hand and return it to the scabbard in the most convenient manner.

If marching or lying down, the bayonet is fixed or unfixed in the most expeditious and convenient manner and the piece returned to the original position.

Fix and unfix bayonet are executed with promptness and regularity but not in cadence.

## The Inspection

**91.** Being at order arms: 1. *Inspection,* 2. *ARMS.*

At the second command take the position of port arms. (*TWO*) Seize the bolt handle with the thumb and forefinger of the right hand, turn the handle up, draw the bolt back, and glance at the chamber. Having found the chamber empty, or having emptied it, raise the head and eyes to the front.

**92.** Being at inspection arms:

1. *Order* (*Right shoulder, port*), 2. *ARMS.*

At the preparatory command push the bolt forward, turn the handle down, pull the trigger, and resume port arms. At the command arms, complete the movement ordered.

## To Dismiss the Squad

**93.** Being at halt: 1. *Inspection,* 2. *ARMS,* 3. *Port,* 4. *ARMS.* 5. *DISMISSED.*

INSPECTION, ARMS

## SCHOOL OF THE SQUAD

**94.** Soldiers are grouped into squads for purposes of instruction, discipline, control, and order.

**95.** The squad proper consists of a corporal and seven privates.

The movements in the School of the Squad are designed to make the squad a fixed unit and to facilitate the control and movement of the company. If the number of men grouped is more than 3 and less than 12, they are formed as a squad of 4 files, the excess above 8 being posted as file closers. If the number grouped is greater than 11, 2 or more squads are formed and the group is termed a platoon.

For the instruction of recruits, these rules may be modified.

**96.** The corporal is the squad leader, and when absent is replaced by a designated private. If no private is designated, the senior in length of service acts as leader.

The corporal, when in ranks, is posted as the left man in the front rank of the squad.

When the corporal leaves the ranks to lead his squad, his rear rank man steps into the front rank, and the file remains blank until the corporal returns to his place in ranks, when his rear rank man steps back into the rear rank.

**97.** In battle officers and sergeants endeavor to preserve the integrity of squads; they designate new leaders to replace those disabled, organize new squads when necessary, and see that every man is placed in a squad.

Men are taught the necessity of remaining with the squad to which they belong and, in case it be broken up or they become separated therefrom, to attach themselves to the nearest squad and platoon leaders, whether these be of their own or of another organization.

**98.** The squad executes the *halt, rests, facings, steps* and *marchings,* and the *manual of arms* as explained in the School of the Soldier.

THE SQUAD

The team of eight.  The team upon which all the work of the company depends.

## To Form the Squad

**99.** To form the squad the instructor places himself 3 paces in front of where the center is to be and commands: *FALL IN.*

The men assemble at attention, pieces at the order, and are arranged by the corporal in double rank, as nearly as practicable in order of height from right to left, each man dropping his left hand as soon as the man on his left has his interval. The rear rank forms with distance of 40 inches.

The instructor then commands: *COUNT OFF.*

At this command all except the right file executes *eyes right,* and beginning on the right, the men in each rank count *one, two, three, four;* each man turns his head and eyes to the front as he counts.

Pieces are then inspected.  (Inspection ARMS).

### Alignments

100. To align the squad, the base file or files having been established: 1. *Right (Left)*, 2. *DRESS*, 3. *FRONT*.

At the command *dress* all men place the left hand upon the hip (whether dressing to the right or left); each man, except the base file, when on or near the new line executes *eyes right,* and, taking steps of 2 or 3 inches, places himself so that his right arm rests lightly against the arm of the man on his right, and so that his eyes and shoulders are in line with those of the men on his right; the rear rank men cover in file.

RIGHT DRESS

The instructor verifies the alignment of both ranks from the right flank and orders up or back such men as may be in rear, or in advance, of the line; only the men designated move.

At the command *front,* given when the ranks are aligned, each man turns his head and eyes to the front and drops his left hand by his side.

In the first drills the basis of the alignment is established on, or parallel to, the front of the squad; afterwards, in oblique directions.

Whenever the position of the base file or files necessitates a considerable movement by the squad, such movement will be executed by marching to the front or oblique, to the flank or backward, as the case may be, without other command, and at the trail.

**101.** To preserve the alignment when marching: *GUIDE RIGHT (LEFT)*.

The men preserve their intervals from the side of the guide, yielding to pressure from that side and resisting pressure from the opposite direction; they recover intervals, if lost, by gradually opening out or closing in; they recover alignment by slightly lengthening or shortening the step; the rear-rank men cover their file leaders at 40 inches.

In double rank, the front-rank man on the right, or designated flank, conducts the march; when marching faced to the flank, the leading man of the front rank is the guide.

AT INTERVALS

## To Take Intervals and Distances

**102.** Being in line at a halt: 1. *Take interval*, 2. (*b*) *To the right (left)*, 3. (*c*)* *MARCH*, 4. *Squad*, 5. (*d*) *HALT*.

At the second command the rear-rank men march backward 4 steps and halt; at the command *march* all face to the right and the leading man of each rank steps off; the other men step off in succession, each following the preceding man at 4 paces, rear-rank men marching abreast of their file leaders.

At the command *halt,* given when all have their intervals, all halt and face to the front.

*Letters in command refer to diagram.

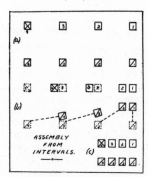

ASSEMBLY
FROM
INTERVALS. (c)

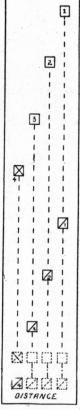

**103.** Being at intervals, to assemble the squad:

1. *Assemble, to the right (left),*
2. *MARCH.*

The front-rank man on the right stands fast, the rear-rank man on the right closes to 40 inches. The other men face to the right, close by the shortest line, and face to the front.

**104.** Being in line at a halt and having counted off: 1. *Take distance,* 2. *MARCH,* 3. *Squad,* 4. *HALT.*

At the command *march* No. 1 of the front rank moves straight to the front; Nos. 2, 3, and 4 of the front rank and Nos. 1, 2, 3, and 4 of the rear rank, in the order named, move straight to the front, each stepping off so as to follow the preceding man at 4 paces. The command *halt* is given when all have their distances.

**105.** Being at distances, to assemble the squad: 1. *Assemble,* 2. *MARCH.*

No. 1 of the front rank stands fast; the other numbers move forward to their proper places in line.

DISTANCE

## To Stack and Take Arms

**106.** Being in line at a halt: *STACK ARMS.*

Each even number of the front rank grasps his piece with the left hand at the upper band and rests the butt between his feet, barrel to the front, muzzle inclined slightly to the front and opposite the center of the interval on his right, the thumb and forefinger raising the stacking swivel; each even number of the rear rank then passes

his piece, barrel to the rear, to his file leader, who grasps it between the bands with his right hand and throws the butt about 2 feet in advance of that of his own piece and opposite the right of the interval, the right hand slipping to the upper band, the thumb and forefinger raising the stacking swivel, which he engages with that of his own piece.

Each odd number of the front rank raises his piece with his right hand, carries it well forward, barrel to the front; the left hand, guiding the stacking swivel, engages the lower hook of the swivel of his own piece with the free hook of that of the even number of the rear rank; he then turns the barrel outward into the angle formed by the other

two pieces and lowers the butt to the ground, to the right of and against the toe of his right shoe.

The stacks made, the loose pieces are laid on them by the even numbers of the front rank.

When each man has finished handling pieces, he takes the position of the soldier.

**107.** Being in line behind the stacks: *TAKE ARMS*.

The loose pieces are returned by the even numbers of the front rank; each even number of the front rank grasps his own piece with the left hand, the piece of his rear-rank man with his right hand, grasping both between the bands; each odd number of the front rank grasps his piece in the same way with the right hand, disengages it by raising the butt from the ground and then, turning the piece to the right, detaches it from the stack; each even num-

ber of the front rank disengages and detaches his piece by turning it to the left, and then passes the piece of his rear-rank man to him, and all resume the order.

**108.** Should any squad have Nos. 2 and 3 blank files, No. 1 rear rank takes the place of No. 2 rear rank in making and breaking the stack; the stacks made or broken, he resumes his post.

Pieces not used in making the stack are termed *loose pieces.*

Pieces are never stacked with the bayonet fixed.

### The Oblique March

**109.** For the instruction of recruits, the squad being in column or correctly aligned, the instructor causes the squad to face half right or half left, points out to the men their relative p o s i t ions, and explains that these are to be maintained in the oblique march.

**110.** 1. *Right (Left) oblique,* 2. *MARCH.*

Each man steps off in a direction 45° to the right of his original front. He preserves his relative position, keeping his shoulders parallel to those of the guide (the man on the right front of the line or column), and so regulates his steps that the ranks remain parallel to their original front.

At the command *halt* the men halt faced to the front.

To resume the original direction: 1. *Forward,* 2. *MARCH.*

The men half face to the left in marching and then move straight to the front.

If at *half step* or *mark time* while obliquing, the oblique march is resumed by the commands: 1. *Oblique,* 2. *MARCH.*

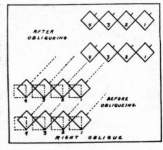

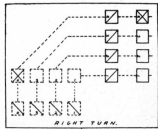

### To Turn on Moving Pivot

**111.** Being in line: 1. *Right (Left) turn,* 2. *MARCH.*

The movement is executed by each rank successively and on the same ground. At the second command, the pivot man of the front rank faces to the right in marching and takes the half step; the other men of the rank oblique to the right until opposite their places in line, then execute a second right oblique and take the half step on arriving abreast of the pivot man. All glance toward the marching flank while at half step and take the full step without command as the last man arrives on the line.

*Right (Left) half turn* is executed in a similar manner. The pivot man makes a half change of direction to the right and the other men make quarter changes in obliquing.

### To Turn on Fixed Pivot

**112.** Being in line, to turn and march: 1. *Squad right (left),* 2. *MARCH.*

At the second command, the right flank man in the front rank faces to the right in marching and marks time; the other front rank men oblique to the right, place themselves abreast of the pivot, and mark time. In the rear rank the third man from the right, followed in column by the second and first, move straight to the front until in rear of his front-rank man, when all face to the right in marching and mark time; the other number of the rear rank moves straight to the front four paces and places himself abreast of the man on his right. Men on the new line glance toward the marching flank while marking time and, as the last man arrives on the line, both ranks execute *forward, march,* without command.

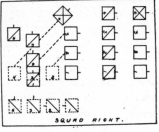

**113.** Squad Right in detail. The front rank has completed the turn.

Squad Right in detail. Execution of the movement by the rear rank.

**114.** Being in line, to turn and halt: 1. *Squad right (left)*, 2. *MARCH*, 3. *Squad*, 4. *HALT*.

The third command is given immediately after the second. The turn is executed as prescribed in the preceding paragraph except, that all men, on arriving on the new line, mark time until the fourth command is given, when all halt. The fourth command should be given as the last man arrives on the line.

**115.** Being in line, to turn about and march: 1. *Squad right (left) about,* 2. *MARCH*.

At the second command, the front rank twice executes *squad right,* initiating the second *squad right* when the man on the marching flank has arrived abreast of the rank. In the rear rank, the third man from the right, followed by the second and first in column, moves straight to the front until on the prolongation of the line to be occupied by the rear rank; changes direction to the right; moves in the new direction until in rear of his front-rank man, when all face to the right in maching, mark time, and glance toward the marching flank. The fourth man marches on the left of the third to his new position; as he arrives on the line, both ranks execute *forward, march,* without command.

**116.** Being in line, to turn about and halt: 1. *Squad right (left) about,* 2. *MARCH*, 3. *Squad*, 4. *HALT*.

The third command is given immediately after the second. The turn is executed as prescribed in the preceding paragraph except that all men, on arriving on the new line, mark time until the fourth command is given, when all halt. The fourth command should be given as the last man arrives on the line.

## To Follow the Corporal

**117.** Being assembled or deployed, to march the squad without unnecessary commands, the corporal places himself in front of it and commands: *FOLLOW ME.*

If in line or skirmish line, No. 2 of the front rank follows in the trace of the corporal at about 3 paces; the other men conform to the movements of No. 2, guiding on him and maintaining their relative positions.

If in column, the head of the column follows the corporal.

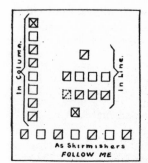

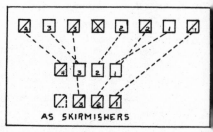

AS SKIRMISHERS

## To Deploy as Skirmishers

**118.** Being in any formation, assembled: 1. *As skirmishers,* 2. *MARCH.*

The corporal places himself in front of the squad, if not already there. Moving at a run, the men place themselves abreast of the corporal at half-pace intervals, Nos. 1 and 2 on his right, Nos. 3 and 4 on his left, rear-rank men on the right of their file leaders, extra men on the left of No. 4; all then conform to the corporal's gait.

When the squad is acting alone, skirmish line is similarly formed on No. 2 of the front rank, who stands fast or continues the march, as the case may be; the corporal places himself in front of the squad when advancing and in rear when halted.

When deployed as skirmishers, the men march at ease, pieces at the trail unless otherwise ordered.

The corporal is the guide when in the line; otherwise No. 2 front rank is the guide.

**119.** The normal interval between skirmishers is one-half pace, resulting practically in one man per yard of front. The front of a squad thus deployed as skirmishers is about 10 paces.

### To Increase or Diminish Intervals

**120.** If assembled, and it is desired to deploy at greater than the normal interval; or if deployed, and it is desired to increase or decrease the interval: 1. *As skirmishers, (so many) paces,* 2. *MARCH.*

Intervals are taken at the indicated number of paces. If already deployed, the men move by the flank toward or away from the guide.

### The Assembly

**121.** Being deployed: 1. *Assemble,* 2. *MARCH.*

The men move toward the corporal and form in their proper places.

If the corporal

continues to advance, the men move in double time, form, and follow him.

The assembly while marching to the rear is not executed.

### Kneeling and Lying Down

**122.** If standing: *KNEEL.*

Half face to the right; carry the right toe about 1 foot to the left rear of the left heel; kneel on right knee, sitting as nearly as possible on the right heel; left forearm across left thigh; piece remains in position of order arms, right hand grasping it above the lower band.

SQUAD KNEELING

**123.** If standing or kneeling: *LIE DOWN.*

Kneel, but with right knee against left heel; carry back the left foot and lie flat on the belly, inclining body about 35° to the right; piece horizontal, barrel up, muzzle off the ground and pointed to the front; elbows on the ground; left hand at the balance, right hand grasping the small of the stock opposite the neck. This is the position of order arms, lying down.

**124.** If kneeling or lying down: *RISE.*

If kneeling, stand up, faced to the front, on the ground marked by the left heel.

If lying down, raise body on both knees; stand up, faced to the front, on the ground marked by the knees.

**125.** If lying down: *KNEEL.*

Raise the body on both knees; take the position of kneel.

In double rank, the positions of kneeling and lying down are ordinarily used only for the better utilization of cover.

When deployed as skirmishers, a sitting position may be taken in lieu of the position kneeling.

## LOADINGS AND FIRINGS

**126.** The commands for loading and firing are the same whether standing, kneeling, or lying down. The firings are always executed at a halt.

When kneeling or lying down in double rank, the rear rank does not load, aim, or fire.

The instruction in firing will be preceded by a command for loading.

Loadings are executed in line and skirmish line only.

**127.** Pieces having been ordered loaded are kept loaded without command until the command *unload,* or *inspection arms,* fresh clips being inserted when the magazine is exhausted.

**128.** The aiming point or target is carefully pointed out. This may be done before or after announcing the sight setting. Both are indicated before giving the command for firing, but may be omitted when the target appears suddenly and is unmistakable; in such case battle sight is used if no sight setting is announced.

**129.** The target or aiming point having been designated and the sight setting announced, such designation or announcement need not be repeated, until a change of either or both is necessary.

Troops are trained to continue their fire upon the aiming point or target designated, and at the sight setting announced, until a change is ordered.

**130.** If the men are not already in the position of load, that position is taken at the announcement of the sight setting; if the announcement is omitted, the position is taken at the first command for firing.

**131.** When deployed, the use of the sling as an aid to accurate firing is discretionary with each man.

## To Load

**132.** Being in line or skirmish line at halt: 1. *With dummy (blank or ball) cartridges,* 2. *LOAD.*

At the command *load* each front-rank man or skirmisher faces half right and carries the right foot to the right, about 1 foot, to such position as will insure the greatest firmness and steadiness of the body; raises, or lowers, the piece and drops it into the left hand at the balance, left thumb extended along the stock, muzzle at the height of the breast, and turns the cut-off up. With the right hand he turns and draws the bolt back, takes a loaded clip and inserts the end in the clip slots, places the thumb on the powder space of the top cartridge, the fingers extending around the piece and tips resting on the magazine floor plate; forces the cartridges into the magazine by pressing down with the thumb; without removing the clip, thrusts the bolt home, turning down the handle; turns the safety lock to the "safe" and carries the hand to the small of the stock. Each rear rank man moves to the right front, takes a similar position opposite the interval to the right of his front rank man, muzzle of the piece extending beyond the front rank, and loads.

A skirmish line may load while moving, the pieces being held as nearly as practicable in the position of load.

POSITION OF LOAD

If kneeling or sitting, the position of the piece is similar; if kneeling, the left forearm rests on the left thigh; if sitting the elbows are supported by the knees. If lying down, the left hand steadies and supports the piece at the balance, the toe of the butt resting on the ground, the muzzle off the ground.

For reference, these positions (standing, kneeling, and lying down) are designated as that of *load.*

**133.** For instruction in loading: 1. *Simulate,* 2. *LOAD.*

Executed as above described except that the cut-off remains "off" and the handling of cartridges is simulated.

The recruits are first taught to *simulate* loading and firing; after a few lessons dummy cartridges may be used. Later, blank cartridges may be used.

**134.** The rifle may be used as a single loader by turning the magazine "off." The magazine may be filled in whole or in part while "off" or "on" by pressing cartridges singly down and back until they are in the proper place. The use of the rifle as a single loader is, however, to be regarded as exceptional.

## To Unload

**135.** UNLOAD.

Take the position of load, turn the safety lock up and move bolt alternately back and forward until all the cartridges are ejected. After the last cartridge is ejected the chamber is closed by first thrusting the bolt slightly forward to free it from the stud holding it in place when the chamber is open, pressing the follower down and back to engage it under the bolt and then thrusting the bolt home; the trigger is pulled. The cartridges are then picked up, cleaned, and returned to the belt and the piece is brought to the order.

## To Set the Sight

**136.** *RANGE, ELEVEN HUNDRED (EIGHT-FIFTY, etc.),* or *BATTLE SIGHT.*

The sight is set at the elevation indicated. The instructor explains and verifies sight settings.

## To Fire by Volley

**137.** 1. *READY,* 2. *AIM,* 3. *Squad,* 4. *FIRE.*

At the command *ready* turn the safety lock to the "ready;" at the command *aim* raise the piece with both hands and sup-

port the butt firmly against the hollow of the right shoulder, right thumb clasping the stock, barrel horizontal, left elbow well under the piece, right elbow as high as the shoulder; incline the head slightly forward and a little to the right, cheek against the stock, left eye closed, right eye looking through the notch of the rear sight so as to perceive the object aimed at, second joint of forefinger resting lightly against the front of the trigger and taking up the slack; top of front sight is carefully raised into, and held in, the line of sight.

Each rear-rank man aims through the interval to the right of his file leader and leans slightly forward to advance the muzzle of his piece beyond the front rank.

In aiming kneeling, the left elbow rests on the left knee, point of elbow in front of kneecap. In aiming sitting, the elbows are supported by the knees.

In aiming lying down, raise the piece with both hands; rest on both elbows and press the butt firmly against the right shoulder.

At the command *fire* press the finger against the trigger; fire without deranging the aim and without lowering or turning the piece; lower the piece in the position of *Load* and load.

**138.** To continue the firing: 1. *AIM,* 2. *Squad,* 3. *FIRE.*

Each command is executed as previously explained. *Load* (from magazine) is executed by drawing back and thrusting home the bolt with the right hand, leaving the safety lock at the "ready."

## To Fire at Will

**139.** *FIRE AT WILL.*

Each man, independently of the others, comes to the *ready,* aims carefully and deliberately at the aiming point or target, *fires, loads,* and continues the firing until ordered to *suspend* or *cease firing.*

**140.** To increase (decrease) the rate of fire in progress the instructor shouts: *FASTER (SLOWER).*

Men are trained to fire at the rate of about three shots per minute at effective ranges and five or six at close ranges, devoting the minimum of time to loading and the maximum to deliberate aiming. To illustrate the necessity for deliberation, and to habituate men to combat conditions, small and comparatively indistinct targets are designated.

## To Fire by Clip

**141.** *CLIP FIRE.*

Executed in the same manner as *fire at will,* except that each man, after having exhausted the cartridges then in the piece, *suspends firing.*

## To Suspend Firing

**142.** The instructor blows a *long blast* of the whistle and repeats same, if necessary, or commands: *SUSPEND FIRING.*

Firing stops; pieces are held, loaded and locked, in a position of readiness for instant resumption of firing, rear sights unchanged. The men continue to observe the target or aiming point, or the place at which the target disappeared, or at which it is expected to reappear.

This whistle signal may be used as a preliminary to *cease firing.*

## To Cease Firing

**143.** *CEASE FIRING.*

Firing stops; pieces not already there are brought to the position of load, the cut-off turned down if firing from magazine, the cartridge is drawn or the empty shell is ejected, the trigger is pulled, sights are laid down, and the piece is brought to the order.

*Cease firing* is used for long pauses to prepare for changes of position or to steady the men.

**144.** Commands for suspending or ceasing fire may be given at any time after the preparatory command for firing, whether the firing has actually commenced or not.

## The Use of Cover

**145.** The recruit should be given careful instruction in the individual use of cover.

It should be impressed upon him that, in taking advantage of natural cover, he must be able to fire easily and effectively upon the enemy; if advancing on an enemy, he must do so steadily and as rapidly as possible; he must conceal himself as much as possible while firing and while advancing. While setting his sight he should be under cover or lying prone.

**146.** To teach him to fire easily and effectively, at the same time concealing himself from the view of the enemy, he is practiced in simulated firing in the prone, sitting, kneeling, and crouching positions, from behind hillocks, trees, heaps of earth or rocks, from depressions, gullies, ditches, doorways, or windows. He is taught to fire around the right side of his concealment whenever possible, or, when this is not possible, to rise enough to fire over the top of his concealment.

When these details are understood, he is required to select cover with reference to an assumed enemy and to place himself behind it in proper position for firing.

**147.** The evil of remaining too long in one place, however good the concealment, should be explained. He should be taught to advance from cover to cover, selecting cover in advance before leaving his concealment.

It should be impressed upon him that a man running rapidly toward an enemy furnishes a poor target. He should be trained in springing from a prone position behind concealment, running at top speed to cover and throwing himself behind it. He should also be practiced in advancing from cover to cover by crawling, or by lying on the left side, rifle grasped in the right hand, and pushing himself forward with the right leg.

**148.** He should be taught that, when fired on while acting independently, he should drop to the ground, seek cover, and then endeavor to locate his enemy.

**149.** The instruction of the recruit in the use of cover is continued in the combat exercises of the company, but he must then be taught that the proper advance of the platoon or company and the effectiveness of its fire is of greater importance than the question of cover for individuals. He should also be taught that he may not move about or shift his position in the firing line except the better to see the target.

## Observation

**150.** The ability to use his eyes accurately is of great importance to the soldier. The recruit should be trained in observing his surroundings from positions and when on the march.

He should be practiced in pointing out and naming military features of the ground; in distinguishing between living beings; in counting distant groups of objects or beings; in recognizing colors and forms.

**151.** In the training of men in the mechanism of the firing line, they should be practiced in repeating to one another target and aiming point designations and in quickly locating and pointing out a designated target. They should be taught to distinguish, from a prone position, distant objects, particularly troops, both with the naked eye and with field glasses. Similarly, they should be trained in estimating distances.

# CHAPTER II.
## BAYONET TRAINING.

**152.** The system of bayonet training herein is taken from "Elements of Trench Warfare" * (See foot note), which was originally taken from the Provisional Manual of Training of the British Army.

Object: 1. To develop alertness of mind, readiness of muscle and the habit of quick obedience to command.

2. To develop the fighting spirt.

### Features of the Bayonet

**153.** To attack with the bayonet effectively requires good direction, strength and quickness, during a state of wild excitement and probable physical exhaustion. The limit of the range of a bayonet is about 5 feet (measured from the opponent's eyes) but more often the killing is at close quarters, at a range of 2 feet or less, when troops are struggling hand to hand in trenches or darkness.

**154.** The bayonet is essentially an offensive weapon—go straight at an opponent with the point threatening his throat and deliver the point wherever an opening presents itself. If no opening is obvious, one must be created by beating off the opponent's weapon or making a "feint point" in order to make him uncover himself.

**155.** Hand to hand fighting with the bayonet is individual, which means that a man must think and act for himself and rely on his own resources and skill; but as in all games, he must play for his side and not only for himself. In a bayonet assault all ranks go forward to kill or be killed, and only those who have developed skill and strength by constant training will be able to kill.

The spirit of the bayonet must be inculcated into all ranks so that they go forward with that aggressive determination and confidence of superiority born of continual practice, without which a bayonet assault will not be effective.

The technical points of bayonet fighting are extremely few and simple. The essence of bayonet training is continuity of practice.

### Method of Carrying Out Bayonet Training and Hints to Instructors

**156.** An important point to be kept in mind in Bayonet Training is the development of the individual by teaching him to think and act for himself. The simplest means of attain-

---

* Elements of Trench Warfare by Captain W. H. Waldron, 29th Infantry. Published by E. N. Appleton, No. 1 Broadway, N. Y. C. Price 75 cents.

ing this end is to make men use their brains and eyes to the fullest extent by carrying out the practices so far as possible, without words of command, i. e., to point at a shifting target as soon as it is stationary, to parry sticks, etc. The class should, whenever possible, work in pairs and act on the principle of "master and teacher." This procedure in itself, develops individuality and confidence. Sharp, jerky words of command which tend to make men act mechanically, should be omitted. Rapidity of movement and alertness are taught by competition in fixing and unfixing the bayonet and by other such quickening movements.

157. As the technique of bayonet fighting is so simple, long detail is quite unnecessary and make the work monotonous. All instructions should be carried out on common sense lines. It should seldom be necessary to give the details of a "point" or "parry" more than two or three times, after which the class should acquire the correct positions by practice. For this reason a lesson or daily practice should rarely last more than half an hour. Remember that nothing kills interest so easily as monotony.

158. The spirit of the bayonet is to be inculcated by describing the special features of bayonet and hand to hand fighting. The men must learn to practice bayonet fighting in the spirit and with the enthusiasm that animates them when training for their games, and to look upon their instructor as a trainer and helper. Interest in the work is to be created by explaining the reasons for the various positions, the method of handling the rifle and bayonet and the uses of the points. Questions should be put to the men to find out if they understand these reasons. When men realize the object of their work they naturally take a greater interest in it.

159. Progression in bayonet training is regulated by obtaining first correct position and good direction, then quickness. Strength is the outcome of continual practice.

In order to encourage dash and gradually strengthen the leg muscles from the commencement of the training, classes should be frequently practiced in charging short distances over the bayonet practice courses.

160. All company officers and noncommissioned officers should be taught how to instruct in bayonet training in order that they may be able to teach their squads and platoons this very important part of a soldier's training, which must be regularly practiced during the whole of his service at home, and during his periods of rest behind the firing lines.

**161.** The greatest care should be taken that the object representing the opponent and its support should be incapable of injuring the bayonet or butt. Only light sticks are to be used for parrying practice.

The chief causes of injury to the bayonet are insufficient instruction, in the bayonet training lessons, failure to withdraw the bayonet clear of the dummy, and placing the dummies on hard unprepared ground.

## BAYONET LESSONS

**162.** *FORMATION.* Intervals or distances are taken as prescribed in paragraphs 109 and 111 I. D. R. (Par. 102 and 104 herein). Bayonets are fixed, paragraph 95, I. D. R. (Par. 90 herein).

**163.** *TECHNIQUE OF INSTRUCTION.* Before requiring the soldier to take a position or execute a movement for the first time, the instructor should show him the position or how to execute the movement, stating the essential elements and explaining the purpose that they serve.

Illustrate the position or movement a second time, requiring careful observation so that the men will be taught to use their eyes and brains right from the beginning.

Now, require the men to assume the position or execute the movement under consideration. Accuracy and expertness will be developed by practice.

Fatigue and exhaustion should be carefully guarded against. They prevent proper interest being taken in the exercises and delay the progress of the instruction.

POSITION OF
ATTENTION
(SEE PAR. 71)

The training consists of five lessons and the Final Assault practice.

### Lesson No. 1

**164.** The First lesson is divided into:

1. The position of *GUARD,* from which the various bayonet attacks are made.

2. The position of *HIGH PORT,* which is assumed when advancing.

3. The *LONG POINT,* which is the normal method of bayonet attack.

4. The *WITHDRAWAL,* which follows the attack.

The position of *GUARD.*

**165.** Being at the Order Arms: 1. *On,* 2. *GUARD.*

Raise the piece with the right hand, throw it to the front. Grasp with both hands, the left at a convenient place above the rear sight so that the left arm is only slightly bent; right hand at the small of the stock and held just in front of the navel. The rifle is held naturally and easily, without constraint, barrel inclined slightly to the left. At the same time the left foot is carried forward to a point in a natural position such as a man walking might adopt on meeting with resistence. The left knee is slightly bent, right leg straight and braced. The right foot is flat on the ground with the toe inclined to the right front.

ON GUARD

**166.** The common faults that will be noted in assuming the position are:

1. The body will be leaned back from the hips, which causes unsteadiness and does not permit quick and aggressive action.

2. The left arm is bent too much, which raises the point of the bayonet too high and produces a certain amount of constraint. The left hand should grasp the piece at such a point that will avoid this defect. A little practice will show the exact place to hold the hand to obtain the maximum effect.

3. The right hand may be held too low and too far back, which has the effect of raising the point of the bayonet and giving a faulty position to the left arm and hand.

4. The rifle may be grasped too tightly with the hands, which produces rigidity and restrains freedom of movement. The left hand merely guides the bayonet in the attack, the right furnishes the power behind the thrust, hence great care should be taken to see that the left arm is not deprived of its freedom of action by gripping the rifle too hard with the left hand.

### The Position of "REST"

**167.** Being at the position of On Guard: 1. *REST*.

The feet are retained at the position of *Guard*. The piece is lowered, arms extended down, and held in the easiest and most comfortable position.

### The Position of "HIGH PORT"

**168.** Being at the position of On Guard: 1. *High*, 2. *PORT*.

Without changing the position of the hands on the piece, carry the rifle so that the left wrist is level with and directly in front of the left shoulder. The right hand is level with the belt.

Practice will be had at the position of *HIGH PORT* with the right hand quitting the piece, it being held approximately in position with the left hand alone. This will be found advantageous when jumping ditches, climbing out of trenches, surmouting obstacles, etc., leaving the right hand free.

HIGH PORT

## THE LONG POINT

**169.** Being at the position of On Guard. 1. *Long,* 2. *POINT*.

LONG POINT

Thrust the point of the bayonet vigorously towards the point of the objective, to the full extent of the left arm, the stock running alongside of and kept close to the right inner fore arm. The body is inclined forward; left knee well bent; right leg braced, and weight of body pressed well forward with the sole of the right foot, heel raised. The chief power in the Point is derived from the right arm with the weight of the body behind it, the left arm and hand being employed to direct the point of the bayonet at the objective.

The eyes must be fixed on the objective. In making the point other than straight to the front the left foot will be moved laterally in the direction to which the point is made. After progress has been made in the execution of the simple point as indicated above, practice should include stepping forward with the rear foot when the assault is delivered.

**170.** The common faults in the execution of the Long Point will be noted as follows:

1. The rifle is drawn back slightly before delivering the point, which makes for a momentary loss of time that may give an opponent the advantage and should be assiduously guarded against.

2. The stock of the piece is held too high, which makes the guiding of the point of the bayonet with the left hand more difficult, and reduces accuracy in delivering the point at the exact spot intended.

3. The eyes are not directed on the point of the attack. This is an error. One that may cause a man to miss his mark. The soldier must realize what this means in hand to hand fighting. The oponent will get him.

4. The left knee is not sufficiently bent, which does not allow the point to be made with the force intended.

5. The body is not thrust sufficiently forward, which reduces just that much the force of the attack.

6. The point is started at too great a distance from the objective to make a hit. Practice must be conducted in making the point until the soldier knows the exact distance at which he will have to start to produce the maximum effect. This distance is between four and five feet.

During the later stages of the instruction the men should also be taught to step forward with the rear foot when delivering the point.

### The Withdrawal After a Long Point

171. Being at the position of Long Point. To withdraw the bayonet. Draw the piece straight back until the right hand is well behind the hip. Immediately assume the position of Guard. If the leverage or proximity of the object transfixed with the bayonet renders it necessary, prior to the withdrawal the left hand is slipped up close to the stacking swivel.

172. In the preliminary instruction all Points will be immediately followed by a withdrawal, prior to assuming the position of guard.

### Progression

173. After the several positions hereinbefore described have been learned, the Points should be made at a definite place on a target, such as the throat, the stomach, the head, etc.

As progress is made, the pause between the point and the withdrawal is shortened until the soldier comes directly to the position of Guard from the point. Proficiency will finally be attained in making a "feint point" at one part of the target and the real point at another, for example: Feint at the head and point at the right thigh; feint at the stomach and point at the neck, etc.

Attacks at a retreating foe should be made against the kidneys, the position of which should be shown to the soldier.

## Vulnerable Parts of the Body

**174.** If possible, the point of the bayonet should be directed against the opponent's throat, especially in hand to hand fighting. The point of the bayonet will easily enter and make a fatal wound on penetrating a few inches. Other and more or less exposed parts are the face, chest, lower abdomen, thighs and the region of the kidneys when the back is turned. Four to six inches penetration is sufficient to incapacitate and allow for a quick withdrawal, whereas if a bayonet is driven home too far, it is often impossible to withdraw it.

As soon as the nomenclature of the positions and movements are learned the men should work in pairs. They should be practiced in pointing in various directions. 1. At the opposite man's hand, which he places in various positions on and off the body. 2. At thrusting rings tied on the end of a stick.

This practice is conducted without word of command, so that the eyes and brain may be trained.

It is not sufficient that a dummy be merely transfixed. Some particular spot on the dummy should constitute the target. Discs or numbers should be placed on the dummy and the men required to point at a distance of about five feet from it and later as they become more proficient, to point after advancing several paces. The advance must be made in a practical manner and the point delivered with either foot to the front.

The rifle must never be drawn back when making a Long Point in a forward movement. The impetus of the body and the forward stretching of the arms, supply sufficient force.

The bayonet must be withdrawn immediately after the Point has been delivered, and a forward threatening attitude assumed by the side of or beyond the dummy.

To guard against accidents the men must be at least five feet apart and the bayonet scabbard should be on the bayonet.

**175.** The principles of this practice should be observed when pointing at dummies in trenches, standing upright on the ground or suspended from gallows. They should be applied at first slowly and deliberately. No attempt must be made to carry out the Final Assault Practice until the men have been carefully instructed in and have thoroughly mastered the preliminary lessons.

## Lesson No. 2. The Parries

**176.** Being at the position of on Guard: 1. *Right (left)*. 2. *PARRY*. The right or left parry is executed by vigorously straightening the left arm, without bending the wrist or twisting the rifle in the hand, and forcing the piece to the right or left far enough to fend off the adversary's weapon. The eyes must be kept on the weapon that is being parried and not on the eyes of the opponent as indicated in our bayonet combat training.

**177.** The common faults in the execution of the parries consist of:

1. Making a wide, sweeping parry, with no forward movement of the bayonet or body in it.

2. The eyes are taken off the weapon that is being parried.

The men should be taught to regard the parry as a part of an offensive movement, namely of the Point, which would immediately follow it in actual combat. For this reason, as soon as the movements of the parries have been learned they should always be accompanied by a slight forward movement of the body.

Parries will be practiced with the right as well as with the left foot forward, preparatory to the practice of parrying when advancing.

### Practice

**178.** Men when learning the parries should be required to observe the movements of the rifle carefully, and should not be kept longer at this practice than is necessary for them to understand what is required, that is vigorous, yet controlled action.

**179.** The men work in pairs with scabbards on the bayonets, one man pointing with the stick and the other parrying it. The position of guard is resumed after each parry. At first this practice must be slow and deliberate, without being allowed to become mechanical, and will be progressively increased in rapidity and vigor.

**180.** Later a point at that part of the body indicated by the opposite man's hand should immediately follow the parry, and, finally sticks long enough to represent the opponent's weapon at the position of guard should be attached to dummies and parried before delivering the point.

**181.** The men must be taught to parry points made at them:

1. By an enemy in a trench when they are themselves on the parapet.

2. By an enemy on the parapet when they are on the trench.

3. When both are fighting on the same level at close quarters in a deep trench.

## The Short Point

**182.** Being at the position of on Guard: 1. *Short,* 2. *POINT.* Shift the left hand quickly towards the muzzle and draw the rifle back to the full extent of the right arm, the butt either upwards or downwards, according as a low point or high point is to be made. Deliver the point vigorously to the full extent of the left arm.

SHORT POINT

**183.** The short point is used at a range of about three feet. In close fighting it is the natural point to make when the bayonet has just been withdrawn after a long point. If a strong withdrawal is necessary the right hand should be slipped above the back sight after the short point has been made.

**184.** By placing two discs on a dummy the short point should be taught in conjunction with the long point, the first disc being transfixed with the latter and 'the second with the former. On delivery of the long point if the left foot is forward, the short point would take place with the right foot forward and *vice versa.*

The parries should be practiced from the position of the short point.

### Lesson No. 4. The Jab or Upward Point

**185.** Being at the position of Short Point: 1. *Jab*, 2 *POINT*. Shift the right hand up the rifle and grasp it above the balance, at the same time bringing the piece to an almost vertical position close to the body. From this position, bend the knees and jab the point of the bayonet upwards into the throat or under the chin of the opponent.

The common faults in this movement are:

JAB POINT

**186.** 1. The rifle is drawn backward and not held sufficiently upright.

2. The rifle is grasped too low with the right hand.

From the position of Jab, the men will be practiced in fending off an attack made on any part of their body by an opponent.

When making a Jab from the position of guard, the right, being the thrusting hand, will be brought up first.

The Jab can be employed successfully in close quarter fighting in narrow trenches or when embraced by an enemy.

## Methods of Injuring an Opponent

**187.** It should be impressed upon the soldier that, although a man's point has missed, or has been parried or his bayonet has been broken, he can, as attacker, still maintain his advantage by injuring his opponent in one of the following ways:

BUTT STRIKE

**188.** BUTT STRIKE I. Swing the butt up at the opponent's crotch, ribs, forearm, etc., using a half arm blow and advancing the rear foot.

This is essentially a half arm blow from the shoulder, keeping the elbow rigid. It can be executed only when the rifle is grasped at the small of the stock.

**189.** BUTT STRIKE II. If the opponent jumps back so that the first butt strike misses, the rifle will come into a horizontal position over the left shoulder, butt to the front. The attacker will then step in with the rear foot and dash the butt into his opponent's face.

**190.** BUTT STRIKE III. If the opponent retires still further out of distance, the attacker again closes up and slashes his bayonet down on his opponent's head or neck.

**191.** BUTT STRIKE IV. If the point is beaten or brought down, the butt can be used effectively by crashing it down on the oponent's head with an over-arm blow, advancing the rear foot. When the opponent is out of distance Butt Strike III can again be used.

**192.** In individual fighting the butt can also be used horizontally against the opponent's ribs, forearm, etc. This method is impossible in trench fighting or in an attack, owing to the horizontal sweep of the bayonet to the attacker's left. The men must be impressed with the fact that the butt must never be used when it is possible to use the point of the bayonet effectively.

**193.** Butt Strikes can be used only under certain conditions and in certain positions. If the soldier acquires absolute control of his weapon under these conditions he will be able to adapt himself to all other phases of close in fighting. For example, when a man is gripped by an opponent, so that neither the point nor the butt can be used, the knee brought up against the crotch or the heel stamped on the instep may momentarily disable him and make him release his hold. When wrestling the opponent may be tripped by forcing his weight on to one leg and then kicking that leg from under him. These methods will only temporarily disable an enemy, who must be killed with the bayonet.

## Practice

**194.** When the men have been shown the methods of using the butt and the knee, they should be practiced by affixing several discs on a dummy and executing combination exercises at them. For example, point at one disc, use the knee on another fixed low down, jab at a third, etc. For practice with the Butt, light dummies should be used to prevent injury to the piece.

## Tactical Application of the Bayonet

**195.** A bayonet assault should preferably be made under cover of fire, or darkness or as a surprise. Under these circumstances the prospect of success is greatest, for a bayonet is useless at any range except in hand to hand fighting.

The bayonet is essentially a weapon of offense to be used with skill and vigor. To await an opportunity for using the bayonet entails defeat. An approaching enemy will simply stand out of bayonet range and shoot down the defenders.

In an assault the enemy should be killed with the bayonet. Firing should be avoided. A bullet passing through an opponent's body may kill a friend who happens to be in the line of fire.

## Methods of Disarming an Opponent

THE STOCK BREAK

THE BOLT BREAK

THE HAND BREAK

# CHAPTER III*

## RIFLE FIRING

**196.** · **The Rifle**

**Its Name:**
U. S. Magazine Rifle, Model of 1903, Calibre .30. Also called U. S. Springfield Rifle, model 1903.

**Weight:**
8.69 pounds. Bayonet weights 1 pound additional.

**Made:**
Springfield Armory, Mass., and Rock Island Arsenal, Ill.

**Calibre:**
.30. That is, its bore has a diameter of 30/100 of an inch measured between the lands.

**Barrel:**
The barrel is 24.006 inches long.

**Rifling:**
The bore is a cylinder with four corkscrew grooves 0.004 inches deep cut into it. The spaces between these grooves are called the lands. The grooves are three times the width of the lands. The grooves and lands have a uniform twist, one turn in 10 inches and give the bullet a spinning movement which keeps it from tumbling in flight.

Abrasives must not be used for cleaning the bore, since the edges of the lands are cut by abrasives and the life of the rifle is materially shortened. The twist given by the rifling causes a drift to the right, which is overcome by the diagonal cutting in the inner sides of the rear sight leaf.

**Life:**
The rifle will still be accurate after 8,000 to 13,000 rounds have been fired. In general, however, 4,000 rounds is usually given as the "accuracy life" of a rifle.

**197. Ammunition:**
The ammunition used is a cartridge consisting of a brass shell, 47 to 50 grains of smokeless powder, a primer (cap), and a pointed "spitzer" bullet.

---

* This chapter prepared by Captain John W. Lang, 33rd U. S. Infantry.

**Bullet:**

The bullet weighs about 1/3 ounce and is composed of a lead and tin composition core in a cupro-nickel jacket. The cartridge complete weighs about an ounce (395.5 grains).

BALL CARTRIDGE CAL. .30.

**198. Clips:**

The cartridges come packed in brass clips. The clips are packed in Bandoleers.

**199. Bandoleers:**

Each bandoleer holds 60 ball cartridges, arranged in 6 pockets each holding two clips. The bandoleer is made of olive drab cloth and has a shoulder strap of olive drab webbing, and a safety pin is provided to afford an adjustment of its length. The bandoleer packed weighs 3.88 pounds. 20 bandoleers are packed in a hermetically sealed box weighing about 99 pounds, packed.

**200. Range:**

Maximum range, 4,891.6 yards—almost 3 miles. To get this range the angle of elevation must be 45 degrees. It takes the bullet 38 seconds to make the flight.

**Powder Pressure:**

The powder pressure in the chamber of the rifle at explosion is about 51,000 pounds per sq. inch.

**Recoil:**

The maximum energy of free recoil is 14.98 foot pounds.

**Penetration:**

| Material | 50 ft. | 100 yds. | 500 yds. | 1000 yds. |
|---|---|---|---|---|
| White pine butts made of 1″ boards 1″ apart.... | 59.98 | 52.8 | 26.36 | 10.48 |
| Moist sand .............. | 10.06 | 14.02 | 16.1 | 13.9 |
| Dry sand ................ | 6.32 | 6.88 | 13.12 | 10.86 |
| Loam practically free from sand ................ | 19.9 | 17.46 | 23.62 | 17.46 |
| Thoroughly seasoned oak across the grain ..... | 34.19 | 31.18 | 14.328 | .... |
| Brick wall ................ | .... | 5.5 | .... | .... |
| Low steel, boilerplate .... | .528 | .40 | .01 | .0 |

Length of Rifle complete, 43.212".
Length of travel of bullet in bore, 21.697".
Width of grooves, 0.1767".
Width of lands, 0.0589".
Velocity at muzzle, 2700 ft. per second.

**201. Rapidity of fire:** 23 aimed shots have been fired in 1 minute with this rifle, used as a single loader and 25 shots in the same time using magazine fire.

Firing from the hip without aim 30 shots have been fired in one minute, using rifle as a single loader and 40 shots in one minute using magazine fire.

**202. The soldier's greatest assets** are his rifle and his ability to use it to the best advantage and with maximum effect.

He may use it to get fire effect; as a handle for his bayonet; or, as a club.

As a fire arm pure and simple we will consider it here. The Small Arms Firing Manual, 1913, says: "The sole purpose of the rifle training for the soldier is to make him a good shot under war conditions and a scheme of instruction will be effective in so far as it tends to produce that result * * * * By means of preliminary drills and gallery practice, the soldier is trained in the fundamental principles of marksmanship."

As a preliminary, the soldier should know his rifle, its parts—how they function, and the limitations and capabilities of his weapon. There are certain parts of a rifle which are most likely to require repair.

**Bolt Stop:**
Worn by continual contact with bolt.

**Cocking piece:**
Nose worn from neglect to keep it lubricated.

**Safety lock:**
Thumb piece knocked off by blow.

**Striker:**
Broken by snapping on empty chamber.

*There are injuries which do not render a piece unserviceable.*
**Bolt:**
The entire flange at the front end may be broken off—except for a small portion opposite the extractor hook which is required to hold, in conjunction with the extractor hook, the empty shell when it is being drawn to the rear for ejection. If all gone, shells must be removed by hand.

**Ejector:**

If the ejector be broken or lost, empty shells may be removed from the receiver by the finger when drawn back by the extractor.

**Safety lock:**

It is merely a precautionary safety device and its absence does not affect the usefulness of the arm.

**Cut off:**

If it be absent, the rifle can be loaded from the magazine, but the magazine cannot be held full in reserve. In single loading with cut off wanting and magazine empty the soldier should load directly into the magazine as otherwise the forward motion of the bolt will be stopped by coming in contact with the follower. Care must be exercised to avoid drawing the bolt entirely from the receiver.

**Floor plate, follower and magazine spring:**

The absence of these parts prevents the use of the magazine but does not prohibit the use of the arm as a single loader.

**Cocking piece:**

If absent piece may be cocked by raising and lowering bolt handle.

**Bolt stop and sleeve lock:**

Not essential.

**203.        Sights and Sighting Drills**

In order to shoot it is necessary that one learn how to use the sights on the rifle.

The bullet as it leaves the muzzle continues for a moment in prolongation of the bore, but certain forces begin to act. These forces are GRAVITY which draws the bullet toward the earth and the retardation caused by the resistance of the air. As the velocity of the bullet diminishes the curve of the trajectory becomes greater.

The trajectory is the path of the bullet in its flight. This trajectory is rigid, that is to say, the curve described by the bullet in flight has the same shape whether the rifle be fired at an angle of 10 degrees with the horizontal, or 20 degrees.

The high initial velocity of the U. S. magazine rifle gives a "flat" trajectory. Low initial velocity will give a more curved trajectory.

**204.** In order to hit a target one must so aim the rifle that the line of flight of the bullet will intersect the line of sight at the target.

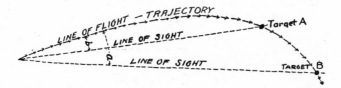

REAR SIGHT LEAF

If the target be very close, the axis of the bore and the line of sight (the line from the eye along the sights to the target) make a very, very sharp angle.

As the distance from the target increases the angle formed by the axis of the bore and the line of sight increases. At maximum range 4891.6 yds., the angle is 45 degrees.

**205.** The angle necessary to be used at the various ranges in order to make hits are automatically set off by using the graduations (reading yards) on the rear sight leaf.

**206.** Uniformity in sighting is vitally necessary if one expects to have uniform results.

Aiming a rifle consists in bringing the target, the front sight and the rear sight into line.

The front sight the top of which is used in aiming, may be considered as a point. The rear sight is either an open shaped notch or a circular peep.

**207.** We will assume that the sight is set at 300 yards at the eye, rear and front sights and the target are in line.

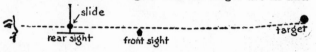

**208.** Now we want to set the rear sight at 1000 yards. If we keep the front sight on the line joining the eye and target and raise the slide on the rear sight leaf to the 1000 mark on the leaf, we will find that the slide is above the line of target.

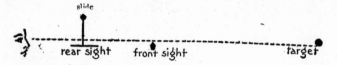

To bring it in line we must lower the butt of the rifle. This is just the same as if we had raised the muzzle. This gives us the angle necessary to have the line of sight and the trajectory intersect at the proper point.

**209.** Open (NORMAL) sight—look through the rear sight notch at the bulls-eye or mark and bring the top of the front sight on a line with the top and center of the rear sight notch and aligned upon the point of aim.

**210. Common Errors:**

Not centering the top of the front sight in the rear sight notch.

Not getting the top of the front sight cover on a line with the top of the rear sight notch.

Combinations of these two:

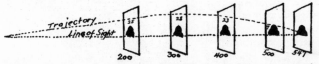

The *normal sight* is used with battle sight.

### 211. Battle Sight:

Is the position of the rear sight with the leaf down. The notch of the rear sight on the slide cap makes the angle of departure 18′ 3.97″—which is the same angle as that obtained with a sight setting of 547 yds. In other words the line of sight and trajectory coincide at 547 yards or the battle sight is equivalent to a sight setting of 547 yards.

In using the battle sight at closer ranges than 547 yards one must aim the piece below the object. This distance below the object varies with the range. At 200 yards it is 25 inches, 28″ at 300 yds., 23″ at 400 yds., 7″ at 500 yards.

**212.** Aiming at bottom of the figure the bullet will pass targets as shown below.

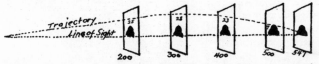

Therefore in order to hit the target at 200 yards using battle sight it will be necessary to aim at a point 25 inches below the point it is intended to strike.

**213.** The position of the slide is not affected by the diagonal groove which is cut in the rear sight leaf to overcome drift. (See page 85) (the rear sight leaf). The slide moves along the outersides of the sight leaf. The drift slide only is affected by the diagonal groove. Since a better aim is secured when the front and rear sights are farthest apart, it is recommended that the slide be at the position closest to the bolt.

### 214. Peep Sight:

The peep sight is the using of the peep hole in the drift slide and the front sight. The eye naturally centers objects. The peep sight is used as follows:

Look through the peep hole at the bull's-eye mark and bring the top of the front sight to the center of the aperture and aligned upon the point of aim.

**215.** Common *ERRORS*—Not centering top of front sight but centering the target.

This error is not important on target range, but in firing in war it is important. Each rifle has a certain sight for setting each range. On the range the bull's-eye is comparatively small and even if centered, the displacement of the front sight is very slight. In battle there would be very little displacement if the target were a prone figure for the objective is small.

If the target be a man kneeling, standing or mounted the error would be great if the target be centered for we would

not be taking a uniform amount of front sight, and in order to hit the target we would have to take a different sight setting for each different size target. This would require a rapid calculation and fine sight adjustive but if we ALWAYS CENTER TOP OF THE FRONT SIGHT we are independent of all factors except range and wind.

### 216. Windage:

In flight the bullet may encounter a wind. If the wind comes from the right the bullet is moved by its force to the left. If the wind be a head wind the bullet is retarded in its flight. A stern wind accelerates the bullet.

To overcome this effect we move the bullet over into the wind the amount we expect the wind to move it, so that the effect of the wind is neutralized. This is done by means of the windage scale on the rear sight. To use it:

1. The direction and velocity of the wind are estimated, either by flags, blades or clumps of grass or some other method.

2. A windage chart is consulted and the amount of windage necessary is set on the windage scale.

To overcome the effect of a 3 o'clock wind (beam wind from Right) we take Right windage which moves the butt to the left and consequently, the muzzle to the right. To raise the shot strike on the target, we raise our sight. To lower it we lower the rear sight and similarly to move the shot strike to the *RIGHT* we move the rear sight to the *RIGHT*.

The "BULL'S-EYE SCOREBOOK" issued by the Ordnance Department and published by the "ARMS and THE MAN", Washington, D. C., has excellent windage charts.

### 217. Canting:

Canting the rifle in firing tends to displace the shot strike and therefore should be avoided. Canting is the revolving of the rifle on the axis of the bore through a small arc. Canting to the right throws the bullet low and to the right.

### 218. What a Rifleman Looks at When He Fires:

The eye can be focused accurately upon objects at but one distance at a time: all other objects in the field of view will appear more or less blurred, depending upon their distance from the eye and from the object upon which the eye is focused.

So we cannot focus the eye upon the rear sight, the front sight and target. We align them, glance from one to another, but *AT INSTANT OF DISCHARGE THE EYE SHOULD BE FOCUSED UPON THE TARGET OR MARK* and *NOT* upon the sights.

### 219. SIGHTING DRILLS

By means of sighting, position and aiming drills and gallery practice, excellent shots may be made without a simple service charge being fired.

**Object of Sighting Drills:**

To teach the proper method of sighting.

To overcome errors in sighting.

To seek uniformity.

The first is taught by means of a sighting bar. The instructor properly sets the sighting bar and calls upon each man to look at it to see what the correct sight is.

The second is taught by requiring men to make triangles, quadrangles, hexagons, etc. A rifle is placed on a rest and sighted roughly at a piece of white paper tacked to a wall. A second man stands at the paper, with a pencil and a disc on the end of a stick. This disc has a black circle on it, and a hole in the center.

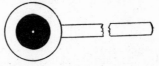

The sighter directs the marker to move the disc up and down, right or left or in any direction and then signals "Mark". The marker makes a pencil mark through the hole and then moves the disc away. When three or more of these in succession are made they are joined and the figure studied.

A pattern like this is excellent.

This shows an error in the amount of front sight taken.

This shows an error in placing the front sight in the center of the rear sight notch.

This shows a combination of the two above faults.

The more compact the pattern—the greater the uniformity.

## ALWAYS CALL YOUR SHOTS

If a shot strikes to the right of the bull's-eye it is called a 3 o'clock 4, 3, or 2.

It it strikes below a 6 o'clock 4, 3, or 2.

If above a 12 o'clock 4, 3, or 2.

To the left a 9 o'clock 4, 3, or 2.

Imagine the target to be a clock face with 12 o'clock up. The center of the bull's-eye at the intersection of the hands of the clock. We can in this manner accurately locate a shot.

Call your shots before they are marked in the pits. This will let your coach know whether you know what you are doing. If you call 9 o'clock and your shots go to the right, he will know that something is wrong and will have to diagnose your case. Probably your error in this case will be due to flinching or to a lack of windage. A glance at your windage scale will tell him which of the two applies.

*CALL EVERY SHOT ALWAYS*

## DISMOUNTING AND ASSEMBLING BY SOLDIER

The bolt and magazine mechanism can be dismounted without removing the stock. The latter should never be done, except for making repairs, and then only by some selected and instructed man.

### To Dismount Bolt Mechanism

Place the cut-off at the center notch; cock the arm and turn the safety lock to a vertical position, raise the bolt handle and draw out the bolt. (Fig. 1).

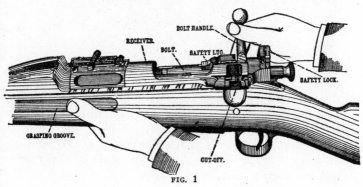

FIG. 1

Hold bolt in left hand, press sleeve lock in with thumb of right hand to unlock sleeve from bolt, and unscrew sleeve by turning to the left. (Fig. 2).

Hold sleeve between forefinger and thumb of the left hand, draw cocking piece back with middle finger and thumb of

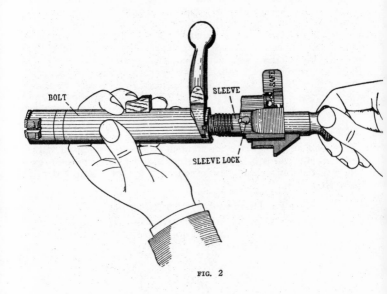

FIG. 2

right hand, turn safety lock down to the left with the forefinger of the right hand, in order to allow the cocking piece to move forward in sleeve, thus partially relieving the tension of mainspring; with the cocking piece against the breast, draw back the firing pin sleeve with the forefinger and thumb of right hand and hold it in this position (Fig. 3) while removing the striker with the left hand; remove firing pin sleeve and mainspring; pull firing pin out of sleeve; turn the ex-

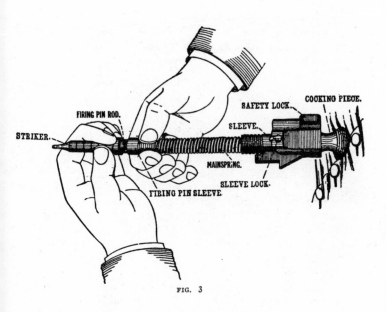

STRIKER.

FIRING PIN ROD.

SAFETY LOCK.

COOKING PIECE.

SLEEVE.

MAINSPRING.

SLEEVE LOCK.

FIRING PIN SLEEVE.

FIG. 3

tractor to the right, forcing its tongue out of its groove in the front of the bolt, and force the extractor forward (Fig. 3) and off the bolt.

## To Assemble Bolt Mechanism

Grasp with the left hand the rear of the bolt, handle up, and turn the extractor collar with the thumb and forefinger of the right hand until its lug is on a line with the safety lug on the bolt; take the extractor in the right hand and insert

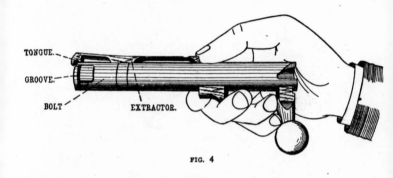

TONGUE.
GROOVE.
BOLT          EXTRACTOR.

FIG. 4

the lug on the collar in the undercuts in the extractor by pushing the extractor to the rear until its tongue comes in contact with the rim on the face of the bolt (a slight pressure with the left thumb on the top of the rear part of the extractor assists in this operation); turn the extractor to the right until it is over the right lug; take the bolt in the right hand and press the hook of the extractor against the butt plate or some rigid object, until the tongue on the extractor enters its groove in the bolt.

With the safety lock turned down to the left to permit the firing pin to enter the sleeve as far as possible, assemble the sleeve and firing pin; place the cocking piece against the breast and put on mainspring, firing pin sleeve, and striker. Hold the cocking piece between the thumb and forefinger of the left hand, and by pressing the striker point against some substance, not hard enough to injure it, force the cocking piece back until the safety lock can be turned to the vertical position with the right hand; insert the firing pin in the bolt and screw up the sleeve (by turning it to the right) until the sleeve lock enters its notch on the bolt.

See that the cut-off is at the center notch; hold the piece under floor plate in the fingers of the left hand, the thumb extending over the left side of the receiver; take bolt in right hand with safety lock in a vertical position and safety

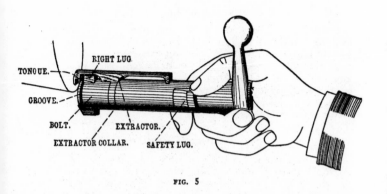

TONGUE.— RIGHT LUG.

GROOVE.—

BOLT.       EXTRACTOR.

EXTRACTOR COLLAR.    SAFETY LUG.

FIG. 5

lug up; press rear end of follower down with left thumb and push bolt into the receiver; lower bolt handle; turn safety lock and cut-off down to the left with right hand.

## To Dismount Magazine Mechanism

With the bullet end of a cartridge press on the floor plate catch (through the hole in the floor plate), at the same time drawing the bullet to the rear; this releases the floor plate.

Raise the rear end of the first limb of the magazine spring high enough to clear the lug on the floor plate and draw it out of its mortise; proceed in the same manner to remove the follower.

To assemble magazine spring and follower to floor plate, reverse operation of dismounting.

Insert the follower and magazine spring in the magazine, place the tenon on the front end of the floor plate in its recess in the magazine, then place the lug on the rear end of the floor plate in its slot in the guard, and press the rear end of the floor plate forward and inward at the same time, forcing the floor plate into its seat in the guard.

220.              Position and Aiming Drills

Purpose: "These drills are intended to so educate the muscles of the arm and body that the piece, during the act of aiming, shall be held without restraint, and during the operation of firing shall not be deflected from the target by any convulsive or improper movement of the trigger finger or of the body, arms, or hands. * * * Systematic aiming and squeezing the trigger will do much to make a rifleman." (Small Arms Firing Manual, Par. 32).

### Position Exercise

**35.** The instructor commands: 1. *Position*. 2. *EXERCISE*. At the last command, without moving the body or eyes, raise the rifle smartly to the front of the right shoulder to the full extent of the left arm, elbow inclined downward, the barrel nearly horizontal, muzzle slightly depressed, heel of the butt on a line with the top of the shoulder.

(Two.) Bring the piece smartly against the hollow of the shoulder, without permitting the shoulder to give way, and press the rifle against it, mainly with the right hand, only slightly with the left, the forefinger of the right hand resting lightly against the trigger, the rifle inclined neither to the right nor left.

(Three.) Resume the position of "Ready."

**36.** *Remarks.*—The instructor should especially notice the position of each soldier in this exercise, endeavoring to give to each man an easy and natural position. He should see that the men avoid drawing in the stomach, raising the breast, or bending the small of the back.

The butt of the piece must be pressed firmly, but not too tightly, into the hollow of the shoulder and not against the muscles of the upper arm. If held too tightly, the pulsations of the body will be communicated to the piece; if too loosely, the recoil will bruise the shoulder. If only the heel or toe touches the hollow of the shoulder, the recoil may throw the muzzle down or up, affecting the position of the hit. While both arms are used to press the piece to the shoulder, the left arms should be used to direct the piece and the right forefinger must be left free to squeeze the trigger.

Paragraph numbers under 220 refer to Small Arms Firing Manual.

## Aiming Exercise

**37.** The instructor will first direct the sights to be adjusted for the lowest elevation and subsequently for the different longer ranges.

The instructor commands: 1. *Aiming.* 2. *EXERCISE.*

At the last command execute the first and second motion of the position exercise.

(Two.) Bend the head a little to the right, the cheek resting against the stock, the left eye closed, the right eye looking through the notch of the rear sight at a point slightly below the mark.

(Three.) Draw a moderately long breath, let a portion of it escape; then, with the lungs in a state of rest, slowly raise the rifle with the left hand, being careful not to incline the sight to either side, until the line of sight is directly on the mark; hold the rifle steadily directed on the mark for a moment; then, without command and just before the power to hold the rifle steadily is lost, drop the rifle to the position of "Ready" and resume the breathing.

**38.** *Remarks.*—Some riflemen prefer to extend the left arm. Such a position gives greater control over the rifle when firing in a strong wind or at moving objects. It also possesses advantages when a rapid as well as accurate delivery of fire is desired. Whatever the position, whether standing, kneeling, sitting, or prone, the piece should rest on the palm of the left hand, never on the tips of the fingers, and should be firmly grasped by all the fingers and the thumb.

The eye may be brought to the line of sight either by lowering the head or by raising the shoulder; it is best to combine somewhat these methods; the shoulder to be well raised by raising the right elbow and holding it well to the front and at right angles to the body.

If the shoulder is not raised, it will be necessary for the soldier to lower the head to the front in order to bring the eye in to the line of sight. Lowering the head too far to the front brings it near the right hand, which grasps the stock. When the piece is discharged, this hand is carried by the recoil to the rear and, when the head is in this position, may strike against the nose or mouth. This often happens in practice, and as a result of this blow often repeated many men become gun-shy, or flinch, or close their eyes at the moment of firing. Much bad shooting, ascribed to other causes, is really due to this fault. Raising the right elbow at right angles to the body elevates the right shoulder, and lifts the piece so that it is no longer necessary to incline the head materially to the front in order to look along the sights.

As the length of the soldier's neck determines greatly the exact method of taking the proper position, the instructor will be careful to see that the position is taken without restraint.

**39.** As changes in the elevation of the rear sight will necessitate a corresponding change in the position of the soldier's head when aiming, the exercise should not be held with the sight adjusted for the longer ranges until the men have been practiced with the sights as the latter would generally be employed for offhand firing.

**40.** The soldier must be cautioned that while raising the line of sight to the mark he must fix his eyes on the mark and not on the front sight; the latter can then be readily brought into the line joining the rear-sight notch and mark. If this plan be not followed, when firing is held on the range at long distances the mark will generally appear blurred and indistinct. The front sight will always be plainly seen, even though the eye is not directed particularly upon it.

**41.** The rifle must be raised slowly, without jerk, and its motion stopped gradually. In retaining it directed at the mark, care must be taken not to continue the aim after steadiness is lost; this period will probably be found to be short at first, but will quickly lengthen with practice. No effort should be made to prolong it beyond the time that breathing can be easily restrained. Each soldier will determine for himself the proper time for discontinuing the aim.

**42.** The men must be cautioned not to hold the breath too long, as a trembling of the body will result in many cases.

**43.** Some riflemen prefer, in aiming, to keep both eyes open but unless the habit is fixed, the soldier should be instructed to close the left eye.

### Trigger-Squeeze Exercise

**44.** The instructor commands: 1. Trigger squeeze. 2. *EXERCISE*. At the command *EXERCISE*, the soldier will execute the first motion of the aiming exercise.

(Two.) The second motion of the aiming exercise.

(Three.) Draw a moderately long breath, let a portion of it escape, hold the breath and slowly raise the rifle with the left hand until the line of sight is on the mark, being careful not to incline the sights to either side. Contract the trigger finger gradually, slowly and steadily increasing the pressure on the trigger, while the aim is being perfected; continue the gradual increase of pressure so that when the aim has become exact the additional pressure required to release the point of the sear can be given almost insensibly and without causing any deflection of the rifle. Continue the aim a moment after the release of the firing pin, observe if any change has been made in the direction of the line of sight, and then resume the position of "Ready," cocking the piece by raising and lowering the bolt handle.

45. *Remarks.*—Poor shooting is often the result of lack of proper coordination of holding the breath, the maximum steadiness of aim, and the squeeze of the trigger. By frequent practice in his exercise, each man may come to know the exact instant his firing pin will be released. He must be taught to hold the breath, bring the sights to bear upon the mark, and squeeze the trigger all at the same time.

46. *The Trigger Squeeze.*—The trigger should be squeezed, not pulled, the hand being closed upon itself as a sponge is squeezed, the forefinger sharing in this movement. The forefinger should be placed as far around the trigger as to press it with the second joint. (See fig. 4, Pl. IV.) By practice the soldier becomes familiar with the trigger squeeze of his rifle, and knowing this, he is able to judge at any time, within limits, what additional pressure is required for its discharge. By constant repetition of this exercise he should be able finally to squeeze the trigger to a certain point beyond which the slightest movement will release the sear. Having squeezed the trigger to this point, the aim is corrected and, when true, the additional pressure is applied and the discharge follows.

## Rapid-Fire Exercise

47. *Object.*—The object of this exercise is to teach the soldier to aim quickly and at the same time accurately in all the positions he will be called upon to assume in range practice.

48. The instructor commands: 1. *Rapid-fire exercise.* 2. *COMMENCE FIRING.* At the first command the first and second motions of the trigger-squeeze exercise are performed. At the second command the soldier performs the third motion of the trigger-squeeze exercise, squeezing the trigger without disturbing the aim or the position of the piece, but at the same time without undue deliberation. He then, without removing the rifle from the shoulder, holding the piece in

position with the left hand, grasps the handle of the bolt with the right hand, rapidly draws back the bolt, closes the chamber, aims, and again squeezes the trigger. This movement is repeated until the trigger has been squeezed five times, when, without command, the piece is brought back to the position of "Ready."

When the soldier has acquired some facility in this exercise, he will be required to repeat the movement ten times, and finally, by using dummy cartridges, he may, by degrees, gain the necessary quickness and dexterity for the execution of the rapid fire required in range firing.

**49.** *Methods.*—The methods of taking position, of aiming, and of squeezing the trigger, taught in the preceding exercises, should be carried out in the rapid-fire exercise, with due attention to all details taught therein; the details being carried out as prescribed except that greater promptness is necessary. In order that any tendency on the part of the recruit to slight the movements of aiming and of trigger squeeze shall be avoided, the rapid-fire exercise will not be taught until the recruit is thoroughly drilled and familiar with the preceding exercises. The recruit will be instructed that with practice in this class of fire the trigger can be squeezed promptly without deranging the piece.

**50.** *Repetition.*—If the recruit seems to execute the exercise hurriedly or carelessly, the instructor wil require him to repeat it at a slower rate.

**51.** *Manipulation of the Breech Mechanism.*—To hold the piece to the shoulder and, at the same time, manipulate the breech mechanism with the proper facility, are learned only after much practice. Some riflemen, especially men who shoot from the left shoulder, find it easier, in rapid firing, to drop the piece to the position of load after each shot. While at first trial this method may seem easier, it is believed that with practice, the advantage of the former method will be apparent.

## The Sling

"The gun sling may be used at all ranges as an auxiliary to steady the piece, in connection with one arm only, provided that for the purposes of adjustment for shooting neither end shall have been passed through either sling swivel. No knot shall be tied in the sling and the sling itself will not be added to nor modified in any manner." (S. A. F. M. par. 91.)

The sling helps to take up the kick (recoil) of the rifle as well as aiding in steadying the piece.

FIG. 6

The sling is made up of two straps each of which has a brass claw hook at one end which is used for adjusting the sling. The short strap D has a swivel through which the long strap B passes. There are 2 Keepers, A and C.

The sling should always be adjusted so that it will be tight. For the majority the long strap should be so adjusted that the loop will come even with the comb of the stock.

FIG. 7

In putting the strap on the arm, grasp the piece at the small of the stock with the right hand, the butt resting against the groin (right groin). Put the left hand in the loop of the long strap from the RIGHT side and twist the sling to the left. Insert the left arm entirely into the loop and grasp rifle at the balance with the left hand and with right hand press keeper down so as to keep the loop as high up the arm as possible. Let left hand, rifle in palm, all fingers grasping the piece slide forward against the upper sling swivel, between the sling and the piece. This twist brings a flat surface against the back of the left hand.

FIG. 8

The sling must be kept well up on the left arm. Many men sew a piece of ½ inch rope on the blouse or shirt to keep the sling from slipping down.

The following figures illustrate the position of the sling and the various firing positions. Study them and pick out those positions that suit your build and tastes.

### Rapid Fire

In rapid fire the piece should be kept to the shoulder while loading from the magazine.

As the bolt handle is raised and pulled back, raise the head and cant the piece to the right slightly and lower the muzzle to the right.

FIG. 9

Keep the butt against the shoulder. Push bolt forward and then down at the same time raising the muzzle to left and lowering the head so that the bolt handle is fully down, the head and muzzle are back in place and the sights may be instantly aligned on the target.

FIG. 10

*KEEP EYES ON THE TARGET.*

Bring the piece to the ready when inserting a new clip.

*HAVE BOLT FULLY BACK.*

Many broken clips result from failure to do this.

Some men prefer to do rapid fire by grasping the knob of the bolt handle with the thumb and first finger and squeezing the trigger with the middle finger. There are advantages and disadvantages in this method.

FIG. 11      FIG. 12

FIG. 13

## Firing Positions

Positions standing:

Body well balanced, feet well apart, planted firmly, left elbow pressed well against the body, head inclined well to right, sling well up on left arm, body in comfortable position thumb along stock.

Note position of left hand. This position gives excellent results in firing, standing. Figure 14 has the following points which should be noted: position of right elbow, inclination of head, position of left arm.

FIG. 14

In Figure 15 the thumb is across the stock. This position in recruits may cause flinching. Recoil carries the rifle and hand back and the thumb, when across the stock is likely to strike against the nose. If this is done repeatedly the recruit begins to dodge the blow and therefore flinches.

FIG. 15

The right elbow, if higher would bring the butt well into the hollow of the right shoulder. This raising of the right elbow tends to reduce the likelihood of resting the butt against the muscles of the upper arm. If the shoulder is not raised it will be necessary for the soldier to lower the head to the front in order to bring the eye into line of sight. Lowering the head too far brings it near the right hand and unless the thumb be placed along the stock a blow may result. Of course the length of the soldier's neck has a great deal to do with the exact method of taking proper position. The thing to bear in mind is—no position should be taken up unless it can be done without restraint.

FIG. 16

Some men keep both eyes open in firing. Unless the habit be fixed in the recruit, it is preferable that he close the left eye.

## Kneeling

Some men desire to sit on the heel.  (Fig. 17).

Others turn the toe inwards and sit on the ankle.  (Fig. 18).

In both cases the left arm just above the elbow rests on the left knee.

Note.  Right elbow should preferably be parallel to ground.

FIG. 17                                    FIG. 18

## Sitting

Note the three positions of the legs and feet in the sitting position.

Note the correct position of sling and of the hands.

FIG. 19

FIG. 20

FIG. 21

### Prone

Note position of legs and feet, sling, left hand and right thumb.

FIG. 22

FIG. 23

SAND BAG REST. The rest shown in (Fig. 24) is the one which produces the best results. There being less dispersion.

With the sandbag rest the difficulty lies in the lack of uniformity in holding the piece. To produce hits closely grouped the piece must be held the same way each time.

Some rifle men prefer (A' or A")

In Fig. 25 the back of the hand rests on the bag. The rifle rests on the hand.

In Fig. 26 the sling is grasped in the left hand and a pull exerted.

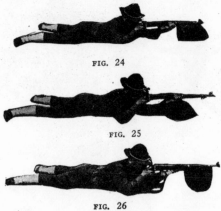

FIG. 24

FIG. 25

FIG. 26

### Placing the Rifle to the Right Shoulder

When the sling is properly adjusted it is somewhat difficult to get the rifle butt in the hollow of the shoulder.

Grasp the butt in the right hand and carry it over to the hollow of the right shoulder.

FIG. 27

FIG. 28

# CHAPTER IV

## PHYSICAL TRAINING

### THE OBJECT OF PHYSICAL TRAINING IN THE SERVICE

**221.** The objects which a course in physical training in the service aim to attain are the development of the physical attributes of every individual to the fullest extent of his possibilities.

These, in order of their importance, may be summed up as follows:

(*a*) General health and bodily vigor.
(*b*) Muscular strength and endurance.
(*c*) Self-reliance.
(*d*) Smartness, activity, and precision.

It is upon the first of these *health* and *bodily vigor,* that the development of all the other qualities so essential in a soldier are dependent, and for that reason the maintenance of *robust health* and the development of *organic vigor* should be considered the primary object of this training.

The tendency of the age is to treat all conditions of health from a pathological standpoint; and while much has been accomplished in the way of increasing the resistive powers of the human organism against the inroads of disease by means of inoculation and other methods of prevention, the development of the inherent power of resistance, which every individual possesses in a greater or lesser degree by means of natural physiological methods, has been much neglected.

It is not sufficient, however, for a soldier to be healthy; his profession demands that he possess more than the average amount of muscular strength and endurance in addition to good health, in order that he may be ready to exchange the comparative comforts of barrack life for the hardships of field service at any moment without diminishing his effectiveness. Hence, the preparatory training he receives must contain those elements that will enable him to do so successfully.

With robust health as a basis and with the knowledge that he is the possessor of more than average strength and endurance, he must be taught how to value the former and how to use the latter to the best advantage. By doing so he will unwittingly develop self-reliance, which, after all, is a physical quality, as it induces men to dare because of the consciousness to do.

Smartness, activity, and precision are the physical expressions of mental activity. All are essential soldierly qualities, as they make for self-respect, neatness, and grace, which combined spell discipline. Precision and exactitude should therefore always be insisted upon in the performance of all exercises prescribed.

In the endeavor to attain the objects referred to above the soldier will be the recipient of a course of training that can not fail to develop him harmoniously, and the liability of developing one portion of his body at the expense of another will be obviated.

## Methods

**222.** In the employment of the various forms of physical training enumerated above it is necessary that well-defined methods should be introduced in order that the object of this training may be attained in the most thorough and systematic manner. Whenever it is possible this work should be conducted out of doors. In planning these methods the following factors must be considered:

(*a*) The condition and physical aptitude of the men.
(*b*) The facilities.
(*c*) The time.
(*d*) Instruction material.

The question of the *physical aptitude* and *general condition,* etc., of the men is a very important one, and it should always determine the nature and extent of the task expected of them; never should the work be made the determining factor. In general, it is advisable to divide the men into three classes, viz, the recruit class, the intermediate class, and the advanced class. The work for each class should fit the capabilities of the members of that class and in every class it should be arranged progressively.

*Facilities* are necessarily to be considered in any plan of instruction, but as most posts are now equipped with better than average facilities the plan laid down in this Manual will answer all purposes.

*Time* is a decidedly important factor, and no plan can be made unless those in charge of this work know exactly how much time they have at their disposal. During the suspension of drills five periods a week, each of 45 minutes duration, should be devoted to physical training; during the drill period a 15-minute drill in setting-up exercises should be ordered on drill days. The time of day, too, is important. When possible, these drills should be held in the morning about two hours after breakfast, and at no time should they be held immediately before or after a meal.

The proper use of the *instruction material* is undoubtedly the most important part of an instructor's duty, for it not only means the selection of the proper material but its application. Every exercise has a function peculiarly its own; in other words, it has a certain effect upon a certain part of the body and plays a role in the development of the men. It is, therefore, the sum of these various exercises properly grouped that constitutes the method. So far as possible, every lesson should be planned to embrace setting-up exercises that call into action all parts of the body, applied gymnastics, apparatus work, and exercises that develop coordination and skill, such as jumping and vaulting.

The best results are obtained when these exercises which affect the extensor muscles chiefly are followed by those affecting the flexors; i. e., flexion should always be followed by extension, or vice versa. It is also advisable that a movement requiring a considerable amount of muscular exertion should be followed by one in which this exertion is reduced to a minimum. As a rule, especially in the setting-up exercises, one portion of the body should not be exercised successively; thus, arm exercises should be followed by a trunk exercise, and that in turn by a leg, shoulder, or neck exercise.

Insist upon accurate and precise execution of every movement. By doing so those other essential qualities, besides strength and endurance—activity, agility, gracefulness, and accuracy—will also be developed.

Exercises which require activity and agility, rather than those that require strength only, should be selected.

It should be constantly borne in mind that these exercises are the means and not the end; and if there be a doubt in the mind of the instructor as to the effect of an exercise, it is always well to err upon the side of safety. *Underdoing is rectifiable; overdoing is often not.* The object of this work is not the development of expert gymnasts, but the development of physically sound men by means of a system in which the chances of bodily injury are reduced to a minimum. When individuals show a special aptitude for gymnastics they may be encouraged, within limits, to improve this ability, but never at the expense of their fellows.

The drill should be made attractive, and this can best be accomplished by employing the mind as well as the body. The movements should be as varied as possible, thus constantly offering the men something new to make them keep their minds on their work. A movement many times repeated presents no attraction and is executed in a purely mechanical manner which should always be discountenanced.

Short and frequent drills should be given in preference to long ones, which are liable to exhaust all concerned, and exhaustion means lack of interest and benefit. All movements should be carefully explained, and, if necessary, illustratled by the instructor.

The lesson should begin with the least violent exercises, gradually working up to those that are more so, then gradually working back to the simpler ones, so that the men at the close of the drill will be in as nearly a normal condition as possible.

When one portion of the body is being exercised, care should be taken that the other parts remain quiet so far as the conformation of the body will allow. The men must learn to exercise any one part of the body independent of the other parts.

Everything in connection with physical training should be such that the men look forward to it with pleasure, not with dread, for the mind exerts more influence over the human body than all the gymnastic paraphernalia that was ever invented.

Exercise should be carried on as much as possible in the open air; at all times in pure, dry air.

All the men except those excused by the post surgeon should be compelled to attend these drills.

Never exercise the men to the point of exhaustion. If there is evidence of panting, faintness, fatigue, or pain, the exercise should be stopped at once, for it is nature's way of saying "too much."

By constant practice the men should learn to breathe slowly through the nostrils during all exercises, especially while running.

A fundamental condition of exercise is unimpeded respiration. Proper breathing should always be insisted upon; "holding the breath" and breathing only when it can no longer be held is injurious. Every exercise should be accompanied by an unimpeded and if possible by an uninterrupted act of respiration, the inspiration and respiration of which depends to a great extent upon the nature of the exercise. Inhalation should always accompany that part of an exercise which tends to elevate and distend the thorax—as raising arms over head laterally, for instance; while that part of an exercise which exerts a pressure against the walls of the chest should be accompanied by exhalation, as for example, lowering arms laterally from shoulders or overhead.

If after exercising, the breathing becomes labored and distressed, it is an unmistakable sign that the work has been excessive. Such excessiveness is not infrequently the cause of serious injury to the heart and lungs, or to both. In cases where exercise produces palpitation, labored respiration, etc., it is advisable to recommend absolute rest, or to order such exercises that will relieve the oppressed and overtaxed organ. Leg exercises slowly executed will afford such relief; by drawing the blood from the upper to the lower extremities they equalize the circulation, thereby lessening the heart's action and quieting the respiration.

Never exercise immediately after a meal; digestion is more important at this time than extraneous exercise.

Never eat or drink immediately after exercise; allow the body to recover its normal condition first, and the most beneficial results will follow. If necessary, pure water, not too cold, may be taken in small quantities, but the exercise should be continued, especially if in a state of perspiration.

Never, if at all possible, allow the underclothing to dry on the body. Muscular action produces an unusual amount of bodily heat; this should be lost gradually, otherwise the body will be chilled; hence, after exercise, never remove clothing to cool off, but, on the contrary, wear some wrap in addition. In like manner, be well wrapped up on leaving the gymnasium.

Cold baths, especially when the body is heated, as in the case after exercising violently, should be discouraged. In individual instances such baths may appear apparently beneficial, or at least not injurious; in a majority of cases, however, they can not be used with impunity. Tepid baths are recommended. When impossible to bathe, the flannels worn while exercising should be stripped off, the body sponged with tepid water, and then rubbed thoroughly with coarse towels. After such a sponge the body should be clothed in clean, warm clothing.

Flannel is the best material to wear next to the body during physical drill, as it absorbs the perspiration, protects the body against drafts and in a mild manner excites the skin. When the conditions permit it the men may be exercised in the ordinary athletic costume, sleeveless shirt, flappers, socks, and gymnasium shoes.

## Commands

**223.** Non-commissioned officers who may be called upon to drill men in the Physical Drill should familiarize themselves with the methods of giving commands as outlined below. As in all other classes of military instruction much depends upon how the instructor goes about his work. There is a right way in the employment of which you will get a maximum effect and a wrong way in which you will get no results. Make it your business to learn the right methods.

There are two kinds of commands:

The preparatory indicates the movement to be executed.

The command of execution causes the execution.

In the command: 1. *Arms forward,* 2. *RAISE; the words Arms forward* constitute the preparatory command, and Raise, the command of execution. Preparatory commands are printed in *italics,* and those of execution in *CAPITALS.*

The tone of command is animated, distinct, and of a loudness proportioned to the number of men for whom it is intended.

The various movements comprising an exercise are executed by commands and, unless otherwise indicated, the continuation of an exercise is carried out by repeating the command, which usually takes the form of numerals, the numbers depending upon the number of movements, that an exercise comprises. Thus, if an exercise consists of two movements, the counts will be one, two; or if it consists of eight movements, the counts will be correspondingly increased; thus every movement is designated by a separate command.

Occasionally, especially in exercises that are to be executed slowly, words rather than numerals are used, and these must be indicative of the nature of the various movements.

In the continuation of an exercise the preparatory command is explanatory, the command of execution causes the execution and the continuation is caused by a repetition of numerals denoting the number of movements required, or of words describing the movements if words are used. The numerals or words preceding the command halt should always be given with a rising inflection on the first numeral or word of command of the last repetition of the exercise in order to prepare the men for the command halt.

For example:

(1. *Arms to thrust.*) (2. *RAISE.*) (3. *Thrust arms upward.*) (4. *EXERCISE, ONE, TWO, ONE, TWO, ONE, HALT*;) the rising inflection preparatory to the command (*HALT*) being placed on the (*"one"*) preceding the (*"HALT."*)

Each command must indicate, by its tone, how that particular movement is to be executed; thus, if an exercise consists of two movements, one of which is to be energized, the command corresponding to that movement must be emphasized.

Judgment must be used in giving commands, for rarely is the cadence of two movements alike; and a command should not only indicate the cadence of an exercise, but also the nature of its execution.

Thus, many of the arm exercises are short and snappy; hence the command should be given in a smart tone of voice, and the interval between the commands should be short.

The leg exercises can not be executed as quickly as those of the arms; therefore, the commands should be slightly drawn out and follow one another in slow succession.

The trunk exercises, owing to the deliberateness of execution, should be considerably drawn out and follow one another in slow succession.

The antagonistic exercises, where one group of muscles is made to antagonize another, tensing exercises, the commands are drawn still more. In these exercises words are preferable to numerals. In fact it should be the object of the instructor to convey to the men, by the manner of his command, exactly the nature of the exercise.

All commands should be given in a clear and distinct tone of voice, articulation should be distinct, and an effort should be made to cultivate a voice which will inspire the men with enthusiasm and tend to make them execute the exercises with wlilingness, snap, and precision. It is not the volume, but the quality, of the voice which is necessary to successful instruction.

## Position of the Soldier at "Attention"

### (See Paragraph 38 for details)

**224.** Assume a natural and graceful position, one from which all rigidity is eliminated and from which action is possible without first relaxing muscles that have been constrained in an effort to maintain the position of attention. In other words, coordination rather than strength should be depended upon.

In the position described (Par. 38), the weight rests principally upon the balls of the feet, the heels resting lightly upon the ground.

The knees are extended easily, but never locked.

The body is now inclined forward until the front of the thighs is directly over the base of the toes; the hips are square and the waist is extended by the erection of the entire spine, but never to such a degree that mobility of the waist is lost.

In extending the spine, the chest is naturally arched and the abdomen is drawn in, but never to the extent where it interferes with respiration.

In extending the spinal column, the shoulders must not be raised, but held loosely in normal position and forced back until the points of the shoulders are at right angles with an anterior-posterior plane running through the body.

FIG. 1

The chin should be square; i. e., horizontal and forced back enough to bring the neck in a vertical plane; the eyes fixed to the front and the object on which they are fixed must be at their own height whenever the nature of the terrain permits it.

When properly assumed, a vertical line drawn from the top of the head should pass in front of the ear, just in front of the shoulder and of the thigh, and find its base at the balls of the feet.

All muscles should be contracted only enough to maintain this position, which at all times should be a lithesome one, that can be maintained for a long period without fatigue.

At the command rest or at ease the men, while carrying out the provisions of the drill regulations, should be cautioned to avoid assuming any position that has a tendency to nullify the object of the position of attention; standing on leg for instance; allowing the shoulders to slope forward; dropping the head; folding arms across chest, etc. The weight should always be distributed equally upon both legs; the head, trunk, and shoulders remain erect and the arms held in a position that does not restrict the chest or derange the shoulders. The positions illustrated here have been found most efficacious.

## STARTING POSITIONS

225. In nearly all the arm exercises it is necessary to hold the arms in some fixed position from which the exercise can be most advantageously executed, and to which position the arms are again returned upon completing the exercise. These positions are termed *starting positions*; and though it may not be absolutely necessary to assume one of them before or during the employment of any other portion of the body, it is advisable to do so, since they give to the exercise a finished, uniform, and graceful appearance.

In the following positions, at the command *down,* resume the *attention.* Practice in assuming the starting position may be had by repeating the commands of execution, such as *raise, down.*

**226.** 1. *Arms forward.* 2. *RAISE,*
(Fig. 2). 3. *Arms,* 4. *DOWN.*

At the command *raise,* raise the
arms to the front smartly, extended to
their full length, till the hands are in
front of and at the height of the
shoulders, palms down, fingers extended and joined, thumbs under fore-
fingers At *Arms, DOWN,* resume
position of attention.

FIG. 2

FIG. 3

**227.** 1. *Arms side-*
*ward,* 2. *RAISE,* (Fig.
3), 3. *Arms,* 4. *DOWN.*

At the command *raise,*
raise the arms laterally
until horizontal, palms
down, fingers as in 1.

The arms are brought
down smartly without al-
lowing them to touch the
body.

**228.** 1. *Arms upward,* 2. *RAISE,* (Fig. 4), 3. *Arms,* 4. *DOWN.*

At the command *raise,* raise the arms from the sides, extended to their full length, with the forward movement, until they are vertically overhead, back of hands turned outward, fingers extended and joined.

FIG. 4

**229.** 1. *Arms to thrust,* 2. *RAISE,* (Fig. 5). 3. *Arms,* 4. *DOWN.*

At the command *raise,* raise the forearms to the front until horizontal, elbow forced back, upper arms against the chest, hands tightly closed, knuckles down.

FIG. 5

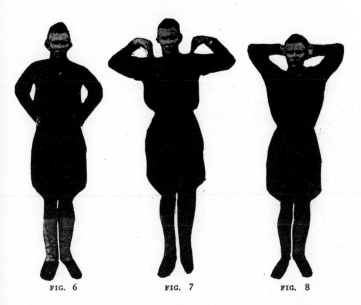

FIG. 6 FIG. 7 FIG. 8

**230.** *Hands on hips,* 2. *PLACE,* (Fig. 6). 3. *Arms,* 4. *DOWN.* (Fig. 6).

At the command *place,* place the hands on the hips, the finger tips in line with trouser seams; fingers extended and joined, thumbs to the rear, elbows pressed back.

**231.** 1. *Hands on shoulders,* 2. *PLACE,* (Fig. 7). 3. *Arms,* 4. *DOWN,* (Fig. 7).

At the command *place,* raise the forearms to the vertical positions, palms inward, without moving the upper arms; then raise the elbows upward and outward until the upper arms are horizontal; at the same time bending the wrist and allowing the finger tips to rest lightly on the shoulders.

**232.** 1. *Fingers in rear of head,* 2. *LACE,* (Fig. 8). 3. *Arms,* 4. *DOWN,* (Fig. 8).

At the command *lace,* raise the arms and forearms as described in 7, and lace the fingers behind the lower portion of the head, elbows well up and pressed well back.

## SETTING-UP EXERCISES

**233.** These exercises form the basis upon which the entire system of physical training in the service is founded. Therefore too much importance can not be attached to them. Through the number and variety of movements they offer it is possible to develop the body harmoniously with little if any danger of injurious results. They develop the muscles and impart vigor and tone to the vital organs and assist them in their functions; they develop endurance and are important factors in the development of smartness, grace, and precision. They should be assiduously practiced. The fact that they require no apparatus of any description makes it possible to do this out of doors or even in the most restricted room, proper sanitary conditions being the only adjunct upon which their success is dependent. No physical training drill is complete without them. They should always precede the more strenuous forms of training, as they prepare the body for the greater exertion these forms demand.

Every preparatory command should convey a definite description of the exercise required; by doing so long explanations are avoided and the men will not be compelled to memorize the various movements.

### FIRST SERIES

**234.**  1. *The Starting Positions.*

    (1)  1. *Arms forward,* 2. *RAISE,* (Fig. 2).

    (2)  1. *Arms sideward,* 2. *MOVE,* (Fig. 3).

    (3)  1. *Arms upward,* 2. *MOVE,* (Fig. 4).

    (4)  1. *Hands on shoulders,* 2. *PLACE,* (Fig. 7).

    (5)  1. *Hands behind head,* 2. *LACE,* (Fig. 8).

    (6)  1. *Arms to thrust,* 2. *MOVE,* (Fig. 5).

    (7)  1. *Hands on hips,* 2. *PLACE,* (Fig. 6).

    (8)  1. *Arms,* 2. *DOWN,* (Fig. 1).

**235.** 2. Arm exercise: 1. *Arms sideward.* 2. *RAISE,* (Fig. 3). 3. *Arms,* 4. *DOWN.*

Two counts: one-two; one-two, etc. Repeat 8 to 10 times.

The arms rigidly extended are brought to the sides smartly without coming in contact with the thighs. Inhale on first and exhale on second count.

**236.** 3. Trunk exercise: 1. *Hands on hips,* 2. *PLACE,* (Fig. 9) 3. *Quarter bend trunk forward,* 4. *EXERCISE.*

Two counts: one-two; one-two. At the count two resume the position of attention. (Fig. 1.) Repeat 8 to 10 times.

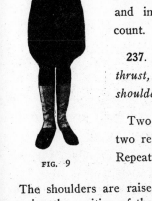

FIG. 9

The trunk is inclined forward at the waist about 45 degrees and then extended again; the hips are as perpendicular as possible; execute slowly; exhale on first and inhale and raise chest on second count.

**237.** 4. Shoulder exercise: 1. *Arms to thrust,* 2. *RAISE,* (Fig. 5). 3. *Raise shoulders,* 4. *EXERCISE.*

Two counts: one-two. At the count two resume position of Arms to Thrust. Repeat 8 to 10 times.

The shoulders are raised as high as possible without deranging the position of the body or head and lowered back to position; execute briskly; inhale on first and exhale on second count.

FIG. 10

**238.** 5. Leg exercise: 1. *Hands on hips*, 2. *PLACE.* (Fig. 6), 3. *Quarter bend knees*, 4. *EXERCISE* (Fig. 10).

Two counts: one-two. At the count two resume the position of hands on hips. Repeat 8 to 10 times.

The knees are flexed until the point of the knee is directly over the toes; whole foot remains on ground; heels closed; head and body erect; execute moderately fast, emphasizing the extension; breathe naturally.

**239.** 6. Foot exercise. 1. *Arms backward*, 2. *CROSS.* 3. *Rise on toes, EXERCISE.*

Two counts: one-two. At the count two resume the position of hands on hips. Repeat 8 or 10 times.

The body is raised smartly until the toes and ankles are extended as much as possible; heels closed; head and trunk erect; in recovering position heels are lowered gently; breathe naturally.

**240.** 7. 1. Breathing exercise: 2. *INHALE,* 3. *EXHALE.*

At *inhale* the arms are stretched forward overhead and the lungs are inflated; at *exhale* the arms are lowered laterally and the lungs deflated; execute slowly; repeat four times.

## SECOND SERIES

**241.** 1. Arm exercise: 1. *Hands on shoulders,* 2. *PLACE,* (Fig. 7). 3. *Extend Arms Forward,* 4. *EXERCISE,* (Fig. 2)

Two counts: one-two. At count two resume the position of hands on shoulders. Repeat 8 to 10 times.

The arms are extended forward forcibly, palms down, and brought back to position smartly, elbows being forced back; exhale on first and inhale on second count.

**242.** 2. Trunk exercise: 1. *Hands on hips,* 2. *PLACE* (Fig. 6). 3. *Bend Trunk backward,* 4. *EXERCISE.* (Fig. 11).

Two counts: one-two. At count two recover to position of hands on hips. Repeat 6 or 8 times.

The trunk is bent backward as far as possible; head and shoulders fixed; knees extended; feet firmly on the ground; hips as nearly perpendicular as possible; in recovering care should be taken not to sway forward; execute slowly; inhale on first and exhale on second count.

FIG. 11

**243.** Shoulder exercise: 1. *Arms to thrust;* 2. *RAISE,* (Fig. 5). 3. *Move shoulders forward,* 4. *EXERCISE.*

Two counts: one-two. At count two recover to position of arms to thrust. Repeat 8 to 10 times.

The shoulders are relaxed and moved forward and in as far as possible and then moved backward without jerking; head and trunk erect; execute slowly; exhale on first and inhale on second count.

FIG. 12

**244.** 4. Leg exercise: 1. *Hands on hip,* 2. *PLACE,* (Fig. 6). 3. *Half bend knees,* 4. *EXERCISE,* (Fig. 12).

Two counts: one-two. At count two recover to position of hands on hips. Repeat 8 or 10 times.

The knees are separated and bent halfway to the ground, point of knee being forced downward; head and trunk erect; execute smartly and emphasize the extension; breathe naturally.

**245.** 5. Trunk exercise: 1. *Hands on hips,* 2. *PLACE,* (Fig. 6). 3. *Half bend trunk forward,* 4. *EXERCISE,* (Fig. 13).

Two counts: one-two. At count two recover to position of hands on hips. Repeat 8 or 10 times.

The trunk is inclined forward until it is at right angles to the legs, hips perpendicular, knees extended; head and shoulders fixed; execute moderately slow; exhale on first and inhale and raise chest on second count.

FIG. 13

**246**. 6. Arm exercise: 1. *Hands on shoulders*, 2. *PLACE*, (Fig. 7). 3. *Strike arms sideward*, 4. *EXERCISE*.

Two counts: one-two. At the count two resume the position of hands on shoulders. Repeat 8 or 10 times.

The arms, knuckles down, hands closed, are flung outward forcibly and brought back to shoulders smartly; execute fast; breathe naturally.

**247**. 7. Breathing exercise: Same as 7 in first series.

## THIRD SERIES

**248**. 1. Arm exercise: 1. *Arms over head*, 2. *RAISE*, 3. *DOWN*. (Fig. 14.)

Two counts: one-two. At count two lower arms with same motion as they were raised. Repeat 8 or 10 times.

The arms, rigidly extended at the elbows, are raised overhead, palms inward, smartly, and brought down the same way; e x e c u t e moderately fast; inhale on the first and exhale on the second count.

FIG. 14

FIG. 15

**249.** 2. Trunk exercise: 1. *Hands on hips, 2. PLACE*, (Fig. 6). 3. *Bend trunk sideward, right and left*. 4. *EXERCISE*, (Fig. 15).

Two counts: one-two. Repeat 6 to 8 times.

The trunk, stretched at the waist, is inclined sideward as far as possible; head and shoulders fixed; knees extended and feet firmly on the ground; execute slowly.

A variation of the exercise is to execute it in four counts, pausing after each, bend to either side, at the upright position.

FIG. 16

**250.** 3. Neck exercise: 1. *Hands on hips, 2. PLACE,* (Fig. 6). 3. *Bend head forward and backward.* 4. *EXERCISE.* (Fig. 16)

Four counts: one—forward; two—recover; t h r e e—b a c k-ward; four—recover. Repeat 6 to 8 times.

The chin is drawn in and the head bent forward, back muscles of neck being stretched upward; shoulders remain fixed; in recovering the muscles are relaxed; execute slowly; inhale and raise chest on first and exhale on second count. In bending the head backward the muscles of the neck are stretched upward; breathe as before.

**251.** 4. Shoulder exercise. 1. *Curl shoulders forward and back.* 2. *EXERCISE.* (Fig. 17).

Two counts: one—curl forward; two—curl backward.

The shoulders relaxed are rolled forward as far as possible, arms being rotated forward; they are then rolled backward and the arms are rotated backward; execute slowly; exhale on first and inhale on second count.

FIG. 17

FIG. 18

**252.** 5. Leg exercise. 1. *Hands on hips,* 2. *PLACE.* (Fig. 6). 3. *Full bend knees.* 4. *EXERCISE.* (Fig. 18).

Two counts: one—down; two—up. Repeat 6 or 8 times.

The knees are separated and bent as much as possible; point of knees forced forward and downward; heels together; trunk and head erect; execute slowly; breathe naturally.

**253.** 6. Foot exercise: 1. *Hands in rear of head,* 2. *LACE,* (Fig. 8). 3. *On toes,* 4. *RISE,* 5. *ROCK.*

Two counts: one—down; two—up. Repeat 6 or 8 times.

The body is raised on toes and then by short and quick extensions and flexions of the toes it is lowered and raised, knees extended; heels together and free from the ground; breathe naturally.

## FOURTH SERIES

**254.** 1. Arm exercise: 1. *Arms to thrust,* 2. *RAISE,* (Fig. 19). 3. *Thrust arms forward,* 4. *EXERCISE.*

Two counts: One—thrust arms forward; two—recover to position of arms to thrust. (Figs. 20-21). Repeat 8 to 10 times.

FIG. 19

The arms, knuckles up, are thrust forward forcibly; in recovering the elbows are forced back; execute moderately fast; exhale on first and inhale on the second count.

**255.** 2. Trunk exercise. 1. *Hands on shoulders,* 2. *PLACE,* (Fig. 7). 3. *Twist Trunk sideward to right and left.* 4. *Exercise.*

Two counts: one—twist to right; two—twist to left. Repeat 6 to 8 times.

FIG. 20

The trunk is turned to the right or left as far possible; hips as nearly perpendicular as possible; shoulders square and head erect; knees extended and feet firm; execute slowly; inhale on first and exhale on second count.

FIG. 21

FIG. 22

**256**. 3. Neck exercise: 1. *Hands on hips*, 2. *PLACE,* (Fig. 6). 3. *Turn head to right and left*, 4. *EXERCISE* (Fig. 22).

Two counts: one—turn to right; two—turn to left. This exercise may also be executed in four counts: one—to right; two—front; three to left; four—front. Repeat 6 to 10 times.

The head, chin square, is turned to the right, or left as far as possible, muscles of the neck being stretched; shoulders remain square; execute slowly; breathe naturally.

**257**. 4. Leg exercise: 1. *Hands on hip*, 2. *PLACE,* (Fig. 6). 3. *Raise right and left knee*, 4. *EXERCISE.* (Fig. 23).

Four counts: one—right knee up; two—down; three—left knee up; four—down. Repeat 10 or 12 times.

The thigh and knee are flexed until they are at right angles, thigh horizontal; toes depressed; the right knee is raised at *one* and the left at *two;* trunk and head erect; execute in cadence of quick time; *breathe naturally.*

**258**. 5. Trunk exercise: 1. *Fingers in rear of head*, 2. *LACE,* (Fig. 8). 3. *Full bend trunk forward*, 4. *EXERCISE.*

Two counts: one—bend forward; two—recover. Repeat 6 to 8 times.

The trunk is bent forward as far as possible; knees extended; feet firm; head and shoulders fixed; execute slowly; exhale on first and inhale on second count.

**259**. 6. Foot exercise: 1. *Hands on hips*, 2. *PLACE,* (Fig. 6). 3. *On toes*, 4. *RISE.* 5. *HOP.*

Two counts: one—up; two—down. Repeat 12 to 16 times.

FIG. 23

The body is raised on toes and the hopping is performed with knees extended; execute fast; breathe naturally.

## FIFTH SERIES

**..260.** 1. Arm exercise: 1. *Arms forward,* 2. *RAISE,* (Fig. 2). 3. *Arms sideward,* 4. *STRETCH.*

Two counts: one—arms forward; two—arms sideward. Repeat 6 to 8 times.

From the front horizontal the arms are extended to their fullest extent and then stretched sideward, the arms rotating till the palms are up; the sideward movement is performed slowly; the recovery relaxed and quick; inhale on first and exhale on the second count.

**261.** 2. Trunk exercise: 1. *Hands on hips,* 2. *PLACE,* (Fig. 6), 3. *Bend trunk right and left forward,* 4. *EXERCISE.*

Four counts: one—bend obliquely to right; two—recover; three—bend obliquely to left; four—recover. Repeat 4 to 8 times.

The trunk is turned to the right and bent forward to the half-bend position, then recover and bend to the left in the same manner; shoulders remain square, in the plane of the ground; head fixed; knees straight; feet firm; hips as nearly

perpendicular as possible; execute slowly; exhale on the first and inhale and raise chest on second count.

**262.** 3. Leg exercise: 1. *Hands on hips,* 2 *PLACE,* (Fig. 6). 3. *Extend right (left) leg forward,* 4. *EXERCISE.* (Fig. 24).

Two counts: one—leg forward; two—recover. Repeat 8 to 10 times.

The knee and ankle are extended forward with a snap, the toes just escaping the ground; all extensor muscles contracted; in recovering relax; trunk and head erect; execute briskly;

**FIG. 24**  breathe naturally.

**263**. 4. Shoulder exercise. 1. *Hands on shoulders, 2. PLACE.* (Fig. 25). 3. *Move elbows forward, 4. EXERCISE,* (Fig. 26).

Two counts: one—forward; t w o—b a c k. Repeat 8 to 10 times.

The elbows are brought together horizontally in front and then forced back as far as possible; the forward movement relaxed, the backward a stretch not a jerk; execute moderately fast; exhale on the first and inhale on the second count.

FIG. 25    FIG. 26

**264.** 5. Trunk exercise: 1. *Hands on hips, 2. PLACE,* (Fig. 6). 3. *Bend trunk forward and backward, 4. EXERCISE,* (Figs. 11 and 13).

Two counts: one—forward; two—back.

Bend trunk forward to the half bend position and then backward; execute slowly; exhale on first, and inhale on second count.

**265.** 6. Foot exercise: 1. *Arms to thrust, 2. RAISE,* (Fig. 5). 3. *Rise on toes, right and left. 4. EXERCISE.*

Four counts: one—rise on right toe; two—recover; three—rise on left toe; four—recover. Repeat 10 or 12 times.

The body is extended on the toes of the right foot and then on those of the left; heels closed; trunk and head erect; execute moderately fast; breathe naturally.

## SIXTH SERIES

**266.** 1. Arm exercise: 1. *Arms upward,* 2. *RAISE* (Fig. 4). 3. *Swing arms downward and upward,* 4. *EXERCISE.* Two counts: one—down; two—up. Repeat 8 or 10 times.

Hold body motionless; do all the exercise with the arms and shoulders.

FIG. 27         FIG. 28         FIG. 29

**267.** 2. Trunk exercise: 1. *Arms over head,* 2. *RAISE.* 3. Fingers, 4. *LACE,* (Fig. 28). 5. *Bend trunk sideward, right and left,* 6. *EXERCISE.* (Figs. 27 and 29).

Two counts: one—right; two—left. Repeat 6 or 8 times.

The arms are fully extended and the body, stretched at the waist, is bent sideward to the right and left; knees straight; feet firm; head erect; execute slowly; breathe naturally.

**268.** 3. Leg and Foot exercise: 1. *Hands on hips,* 2. *PLACE,* (Fig. 6). 3. *To squatting position,* 4. *BEND.* 5. *On knees,* 6. *ROCK.*

Two counts: For rocking on knees. Repeat 6 or 8 times.

The knees are bent in Fig. 18; extend and bend the knees in quick succession; trunk and head erect; heels closed; execute moderately fast; breathe naturally.

**269.** 4. Shoulder exercise: 1. *Arms to thrust,* 2. *RAISE,* (Fig. 5). 3. *Move shoulders forward, up, back, down,* 4. *EXERCISE.*

Four counts: one—forward; two—up; three—black; four—down. Repeat 8 or 10 times.

The shoulders are relaxed and brought forward; in that position they are raised; then they are forced back without lowering them; and then they are dropped back to position; execute slowly; exhale on the first; inhale on the second and third and exhale on the last count.

**270.** 5. Arm exercise: 1. *Arms to thrust,* 2. *RAISE,* (Fig. 5). 3. *Swing arms forward, sideward, forward and back to position.* 4. *EXERCISE.*

Four counts: one—swing forward; two—sideward; three—forward; four—back to position of arms to thrust.

The arms are thrust forward, then relaxed and swung sideward, then forward and finally brought back to position, pressing elbows well to the rear; execute moderately fast; exhale on the first and third and inhale on the second and fourth counts.

**271.** 6. Arm and Leg exercise: 1. *To side straddle swing arms over head,* 2. *HOP.* 3. *RECOVER.*

Two counts: one—hop; two—recover. Repeat 8 or 10 times.

The distance between the legs is about 30 inches; in alighting the toes come in contact with the ground first and knees are bent slightly; trunk and head erect; arms extended; execute moderately fast; breathe naturally.

**272.** The Breathing exercise explained in the First Series, should form a part of the drill at the end of every series.

## MISCELLANEOUS

**273.** 1. Leg and Arm exercise: 1. *Hands on hips,* 2. *PLACE,* (Fig. 6). 3. *Full bend knees and extend arms sideward.* 4. *EXERCISE.* (Fig. 30).

Two counts: one—knees to full bend and arms extended sideward forcibly. Two—recover to standing position with hands on hips. Repeat 6 to 8 times.

Execute moderately slow; breathe naturally.

FIG. 30

FIG. 31                    FIG. 32

FIG. 33

**274**. 2. The leaning rest. 1. *Knees full bend, hands on ground*, 2. *DOWN*, (Fig. 31). 3. *To leaning rest*, 4. *EXTEND*, (Fig. 32 and 33).

Four counts: one—knees bent to squatting position with hands on the ground; two—legs thrown back to the leaning rest; three—recover to one; four—recover to position of attention.

Hands should be directly under shoulders; back arched; knees straight; head fixed; execute moderately fast; breathe naturally.

**275.** 3. Arm Exercise: 1. *Arms sideward,* 2. *RAISE,* (Fig. 2). 3. *Bend trunk right and left,* 4. *EXERCISE,* (Figs. 34 and 35).

Four counts: one—the trunk is bent to the right, the left arm, palm down, is extended obliquely upward and the right arm obliquely downward; two—the body is bent to the left; three—to the right; four—the starting position is resumed; arms extended; knees straight; head fixed; execute moderately fast; breathe naturally.

FIG. 34       FIG. 35

**276.** 4. Trunk exercise: 1. *Arms upward,* 2. *RAISE,* (Fig. 37). 3. *Bend right and left knee, clasp thigh.* 4. *EXERCISE.* (Figs. 36 and 38).

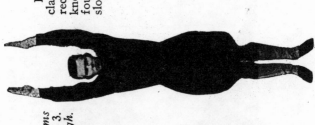

FIG. 37

Four counts: one—bend right knee, clasp right thigh. (Fig. 36); two—recover, (Fig. 37); three—bend left knee, clasp left thigh, (Fig. 38); four—recover, (Fig. 37); moderately slow; breathe naturally.

FIG. 38

FIG. 39   FIG. 40   FIG. 41   FIG. 42   FIG. 43   FIG. 44   FIG. 45

**277.** 5. Arm exercise: 1. *Arms in sequence over head,* 2. EXERCISE.

8 counts: one—right arm up, (Fig. 39); two—left arm up, (Fig. 40); three—right arm over head, (Fig. 41); four—left arm over head, (Fig. 42); five—right arm down, (Fig. 43); six—left arm down, (Fig. 44); seven—right arm down, (Fig. 45); eight—left arm down, resuming position of attention.

**278.** 6. Trunk exercise: 1. *Arms upward,* 2. *RAISE,* (Fig. 4). 3. *Fingers,* 4. *LACE,* (Fig. 46). 5. *Bend trunk forward.* 6. *EXERCISE,* (Fig. 47).

FIG. 46

Two counts: one—bend forward; two—recover. Repeat 6 to 8 times, moderately slow; exhale on one; inhale on two.

FIG. 47

# CHAPTER V

## THE INFANTRY PACK

**279.** The American soldier's pack is the result of an exhaustive study of the subject made by a board of officers of the Army. It was adopted by the Government in 1910. It is essentially an American institution, original in design and construction. It is based upon American ideas of how the American Indian squaw carries her papoose and how the American woodsman carries his load.

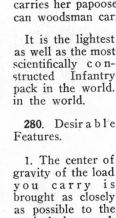

It is the lightest as well as the most scientifically constructed Infantry pack in the world. in the world.

**280.** Desirable Features.

1. The center of gravity of the load you carry is brought as closely as possible to the vertical through your own center of gravity.

2. The load is hung upon the framework (skeleton), so as to economize muscular effort to hold it in place or maintain equilibrium.

**THE ORIGINAL IDEA**

**HOW APPLIED NOW**

3. A reduction to a minimum of pressure upon or constriction of any of the soft parts of the body, large blood vessels or nerves.

4. It eliminates all obstacles to the full expansion of your chest, thus giving free play to your lungs and heart.

5. The load is arranged so that there will be no interference with the free use of your arms and legs.

**281.** The degree of comfort with which you will carry the pack depends entirely upon the manner in which you prepare it and adjust it to your body. There is a right way and a wrong way. Get your's right. It will pay you large dividends in comfort and efficiency.

**282.** There are two methods of preparing the roll. (a) when rations are not carried the "long roll" is made up; (b) when rations are carried the "short roll" is made up. The length of the folded blanket is the determining factor in the length of the roll. It is rolled the long way for the long roll and the short way for the short roll.

**283.** Contents of roll when the long roll is made up.

One Shelter tent half; one shelter tent pole (when provided); five shelter tent pins; one shelter tent guy rope; one poncho; one blanket; one condiment can; one bacon can; one pair drawers; one undershirt; two pairs of socks; one towel; one cake of soap (in a soap box); one comb and one toothbrush.

**284.** When rations are carried and the short roll is made up, the following articles are carried in the haversack instead of in the roll itself: one condiment can, containing coffee, sugar, salt and pepper; the bacon can containing the meat ration; the underwear, the socks and the toilet articles.

## How to Make Up the Pack

**285.** 1. Spread the shelter tent half on the ground. Fold in the triangular end (or ends) forming an approximate square.

2. Fold the poncho once along its long dimension then twice across its long dimension and lay it on top of the shelter half about 8 inches below the upper (button) edge.

3. Fold the blanket the same way as the poncho and lay it on top of the poncho.

4. Arrange the remaining items of the contents along the edge of the blanket, having the condiment can inside t he bacon can and placed at one end to form a solid foundation against which to tighten up the bottom strap of the carrier.

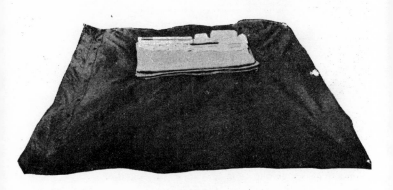

THE CONTENTS OF THE PACK LAID OUT READY TO ROLL.

5. Fold the two sides of the shelter half over the ends of the blanket. Fold the near edge over these, then fold up about 8 inches of the far edge to form the envelope.

READY TO ROLL

Now, rolling the pack is a two-man job. Get your bunkie to help you and you can help him. You will find the task much easier if the two of you work together.

6. Begin on the near side and roll the pack just as tight as you possibly can. Take care that nothing slips.

7. As you near the far end of the roll, open up the fold and roll the pack into it thus forming an envelope. This prevents the pack from slipping.

ROLLING THE ROLL INTO THE ENVELOPE

THE COMPLETED ROLL

8. To make the short roll for the Pack when rations are carried, the process is the same except that the roll is rolled the short way of the blanket.

### To Put the Pack in the Carrier

**287.** Spread the carrier with the haversack attached on the ground and lay the pack on same. Top of pack even with the top of the haversack flaps.

2. Fold over the straps and tighten them. Great care should be taken to get the lowest strap pulled up tight. If this strap should become loose you may as well unpack.

SHORT ROLL WITH
RATIONS

A MARCHING SONG
To the tune of Tipperrary.

**288.**

It's the long roll that's sci-
en-tif-ic,
It's the long roll that fits,
Up and down your spinal
column,
From your shoulders to
your hips.
Thirty-nine pounds Stewart
tells us,
And you've missed some
darn good fun,
If you've never hiked along
the highway,
With this sci'n-tif-ic Ton.

LONG ROLL WITH-
OUT RATIONS

# CHAPTER VI

## TENT PITCHING

### SHELTER TENTS

[For Infantry Equipment, model of 1910.]

**289.** Being in line or in column of platoons, the captain commands: *FORM FOR SHELTER TENTS.*

The officers, first sergeant, and guides fall out; the cooks form a file on the flank of the company nearest the kitchen, the first sergeant and right guide fall in, forming the right file of the company; blank files are filled by the file closers or by men taken from the front rank; the remaining guide, or guides, and file closers form on a convenient flank.

Before forming column of platoons, preparatory to pitching tents, the company may be redivided into two or more platoons, regardless of the size of each.

**290.** The captain then causes the company to take intervals as described in the School of the Squad and commands: *PITCH TENTS.*

At the command *pitch tents,* each man steps off obliquely to the right with the right foot and lays his rifle on the ground, the butt of the rifle near the toe of the right foot, muzzle to the front, barrel to the left, and steps back into his place, each front rank man then draws his bayonet and sticks it in the ground by the outside of the right heel.

Equipments are unslung, packs opened, shelter half and pins removed; each man then spreads his shelter half, small triangle to the rear, flat upon the ground the tent is to occupy, the rear rank man's half on the right. The halves are then buttoned together; the guy loops at both ends of the lower half are passed through the buttonholes provided in the lower and upper halves; the whipped end of the guy rope is then

THE HALVES ARE BUTTONED TOGETHER

passed through both guy loops and secured, this at both ends of the tent. Each front rank man inserts the muzzle of his rifle under the front end of the ridge and holds the rifle upright, sling to the front, heel of butt on the ground beside the bayonet. His rear rank man pins down the front corners of the tent on the line of bayonets, stretching the tent taut; he then inserts a pin in the eye of the front guy rope and drives the pin at such a distance in front of the rifle as to hold the rope taut; both men go to the rear of the tent, each pins down a corner, stretching the sides and rear of the tent before securing; the rear rank man then inserts an intrenching tool, or a bayonet in its scabbard, under the rear end of

PINNING DOWN THE FRONT OF THE TENT

the ridge inside the tent, the front rank man pegging down the end of the rear guy ropes; the rest of the pins are then driven by both men, the rear rank man working on the right.

NOTE.—*The use of the hand ax and the pick mattock in organizations equipped with the intrenching tool is authorized for the purpose of driving shelter tent pins. The use of the bayonet for that purpose is prohibited.*

The front flaps of the tent are not fastened down, but thrown back on the tent.

As soon as the tent is pitched each man arranges his equipment and the contents of his pack in the tent and stands at attention in front of his own half on line with the front guy-rope pin.

**PINNING DOWN THE REAR OF THE TENT**

Both men go to the rear of the tent, the rear rank man holds the pole while the front rank man does the pinning down.

To have a uniform slope when the tents are pitched, the guy ropes should all be of the same length.

*This may be accomplished by putting the front guy rope pin in exactly the length of a rifle from the front pole of the tent.*

In shelter-tent camps, in localities where suitable material is procurable, tent poles may be improvised and used in lieu of the rifle and bayonet or intrenching tool as supports for the shelter tent.

**291.** When the pack is not carried the company is formed for shelter tents, intervals are taken, arms are laid aside or on the ground, the men are dismissed and proceed to the wagon, secure their packs, return to their places, and pitch tents as heretofore described.

The Front rank man holds the pole while the rear rank man pins down the front of the tent.

**292.** Variation with old model Equipment, where a tent pole is used instead of using the rifle.

All unsling and open and take out the shelter half, poles, and pins. Each then spreads his shelter half, triangle to the rear, flat upon the ground the tent is to occupy, rear rank man's half on the right. The halves are then buttoned together. Each front rank man joins his pole, inserts the top in the eyes of the halves, and holds the pole upright beside the bayonet placed in the ground; his rear rank man, using the pins in front, pins down the front corners of the tent on the line of bayonets, stretching the canvas taut; he then inserts a pin in the eye of the rope and drives the pin at such distance in front of the pole as to hold the rope taut. Both then go to the rear of the tent; the rear rank man adjusts the pole and the front rank man drives the pins. The rest of the pins are then driven by both men, the rear rank man working on the right.

## To Strike Tents

**293.** The men standing in front of their tents: STRIKE TENTS.

Equipments and rifles are removed from the tent; the tents are lowered, packs made up, and equipments slung, and the men stand at attention in the places originally occupied after taking intervals.

**294.** Double shelter tents may be pitched by first pitching one tent as heretofore described, then pitching a second tent against the opening of the first, using one rifle or *tent pole* to support both tents, and passing the front guy ropes over and down the sides of the opposite tents. The front corner of one tent is not pegged down, but is thrown back to permit an opening into the tent.

### Single Sleeping Bag

**295.** Spread the poncho on the ground, buttoned end at the feet, buttoned side to the left; fold the blanket once across its short dimension and lay it on the poncho, folded side along the right side of the poncho; tie the blanket together along the left side by means of the tapes provided; fold the left half of the poncho over the blanket and button it together along the side and bottom.

## Double Sleeping Bag

**296.** Spread one poncho on the ground, buttoned end at the feet, buttoned side to the left; spread the blankets on top of the poncho; tie the edges of the blankets together with the tapes provided; spread a second poncho on top of the blankets, buttoned end at the feet, buttoned side to the right; button the two ponchos together along both sides and across the end.

## To Pitch All Types of Army Tents, Except Shelter and Conical Wall Tents

**297.** To pitch all types of Army tents, except shelter and conical wall tents: Mark line of tents by driving a wall pin on the spot to be occupied by the right (or left) corner of each tent. For pyramidal tents the interval between adjacent pins should be about 30 feet, which will give a passage of 2 feet between tents. Spread tripod on the ground where the center of tent is to be, if tripod is used. Spread the tent on the ground to be occupied, door to the front, and place the right (or left) front wall loop over the pin. The door (or doors, if more than one) being fastened and held together at the bottom, the left (or right) corner wall loop is carried to the left (or right) as far as it will go and a wall pin driven through it, the pin being placed in line with the right (or left) corner pins already driven. At the same time the rear corner wall loops are pulled to the rear and outward so that the rear wall of the tent is stretched to complete the rectangle. Wall pins are then driven through these loops. Each corner pin should be directly in rear of the corresponding front corner pin, making a rectangle. Unless the canvas be wet, a small amount of slack should be allowed before the corner pins are driven. According to the size of the tent, one or two men, crawling under the tent if necessary, fit each pole or ridge or upright into the ring or ridge-pole holes, and such accessories as hood, fly, and brace ropes are adjusted. If a tripod be used an additional man will go under the tent to adjust it. The tent, steadied by the remaining men, one at each corner guy rope, will then be raised. If the tent is a ward or storage type, corner poles will now be placed at the four corners. The four corner guy ropes are then placed over the lower notches of the large pins driven in prolongation of the diagonals at such distance as to hold the walls and ends of the tent vertical and smooth when the guy ropes are drawn taut. A wall pin is then driven through each remaining wall loop and a large pin for each guy rope is driven in line with the corner guy pins already driven. The guy ropes of the tent are placed over the lower notches, while the guy ropes of the fly are placed over the upper notches, and are then drawn taut. Brace ropes when used, are then secured to stakes or pins suitably placed.

## Conical Wall Tent

**298.** Drive the door pin and center pin 8 feet 3 inches apart. Using the hood lines, with center pin as center, describe two concentric circles with radii 8 feet 3 inches and 11 feet 3 inches. In the outer circle drive two door guy pins 3 feet apart. At intervals of about 3 feet drive the other guy pins.

In other respects conical tents are erected practically as in the case of pyramidal tents.

## To Strike Common, Wall, Pyramidal, and Conical Wall Tents

**299.** *STRIKE TENTS.*

The men first remove all pins except those of the four corner guy ropes, or the four quadrant guy ropes in the case of the conical wall tent. The pins are neatly piled or placed in their receptacle.

One man holds each guy, and when the ground is clear the tent is lowered, folded, or rolled and tied, the poles or tripod and pole fastened together, and the remaining pins collected.

## To Fold Tents

**300.** For folding common, wall, hospital, and storage tents: Spread the tent flat on the ground, folded at the ridge so that bottoms of side walls are even, ends of tent forming triangles to the right and left; fold the triangular ends of the tent in toward the middle, making it rectangular in shape; fold the top over about 9 inches; fold the tent in two by carrying the top fold over clear to the foot; fold again in two from the top to the foot; throw all guys on tent except the second from each end; fold the ends in so as to cover about two-thirds of the second cloths; fold the left end over to meet the turned-in edge of the right end, then fold the right end over the top, completing the bundle; tie with the two exposed guys.

## Method of Folding Pyramidal Tent

The tent is thrown toward the rear and the back wall and roof canvas pulled out smooth. This may be most easily accomplished by leaving the rear-corner wall pins in the ground with the wall loops attached, one man at each rear-corner guy, and one holding the square iron in a perpendicular position and pulling the canvas to its limit away from the former front of the tent. This leaves the three remaining sides of the tent on top of the rear side, with the door side in the middle.

Now carry the right-front corner over and lay it on the left-rear corner. Pull all canvas smooth, throw guys toward square iron, and pull bottom edges even. Then take the right-front corner and return to the right, covering the right-rear corner. This folds the right side of the tent on itself, with the crease in the middle and under the front side of tent.

Next carry the left-front corner to the right and back as described above; this when completed will leave the front and rear sides of the tent lying smooth and flat and the two side walls folded inward, each on itself.

Place the hood in the square iron which has been folded downward toward the bottom of the tent, and continue to fold around the square iron as a core, pressing all folds down flat and smooth and compactly and parallel with the bottom of the tent. If each fold is compactly made and the canvas kept smooth, the last fold will exactly cover the lower edge of the canvas. Lay all exposed guys along the folded canvas except the two on the center width, which should be pulled out and away from bottom edge to their extreme length for tying. Now, beginning at one end, fold toward the center on the first seam (that joining the first and second widths) and fold again toward the center, so that the already folded canvas will come to within about 3 inches of the middle width. Then fold over to the opposite edge of middle width of canvas. Then begin folding from opposite end, folding the first width in half, then making a second fold to come within about 4 or 5 inches of that already folded; turn this fold entirely over that already folded. Take the exposed guys and draw them taut across each other, turn bundle over on the under guy, cross guys on top of bundle, drawing tight. Turn bundle over on the crossed guys and tie lengthwise.

When properly tied and pressed together this will make a package 11 by 23 by 34 inches, requiring about 8,855 cubic inches to store or pack.

# CHAPTER VII

## COMPANY INSPECTION

**301.** Being in line at a halt: 1. *Open ranks,* 2. *MARCH.*

At the command *march* the front rank executes right dress; the rear rank and the file closers march backward 4 steps, halt, and execute right dress; the lieutenants pass around their respective flanks and take post, facing to the front, 3 paces in front of the center of their respective platoons. The captain aligns the front rank, rear rank, and file closers, takes post 3 paces in front of the right guide, facing to the left, and commands: 1. *FRONT,* 2. *PREPARE FOR INSPECTION.*

At the second command the lieutenants carry saber; the captain returns saber and inspects them, after which they face about, order saber, and stand at ease; upon the completion of the inspection they carry saber, face about, and order saber. The captain may direct the lieutenants to accompany or assist him, in which case they return saber and, at the close of the inspection, resume their posts in front of the company, draw and carry saber.

Having inspected the lieutenants, the captain proceeds to the right of the company. Each man, as the captain approaches him, executes *inspection arms.*

The captain takes the piece, grasping it with his right hand just above the rear sight, the man dropping his hands. The captain inspects the piece, and, with the hand and piece in the same position as in receiving it, hands it back to the man, who takes it with the left hand at the balance and executes *order arms.*

As the captain returns the piece the next man executes *inspection arms,* and so on through the company.

Should the piece be inspected without handling, each man executes *order arms* as soon as the captain passes to the next man.

The inspection is from right to left in front, and from left to right in rear, of each rank and of the line of file closers.

When approached by the captain the first sergeant executes *inspection saber*. Enlisted men armed with the pistol execute *inspection pistol* by drawing the pistol from the holster and holding it diagonally across the body, barrel up, and 6 inches in front of the neck, muzzle pointing up and to the left. The pistol is returned to the holster as soon as the captain passes.

Upon completion of the inspection the captain takes post facing to the left in front of the right guide and on line with the lieutenants and commands: 1. *Close ranks,* 2. *MARCH.*

At the command *march* the lieutenants resume their posts in line; the rear rank closes to 40 inches, each man covering his file leader; the file closers close to 2 paces from the rear rank.

**302.** If the company is dismissed, rifles are put away. In quarters, headdress and accouterments are removed and the men stand near their respective bunks; in camp they stand covered, but without accouterments, in front of their tents.

If the personal field equipment has not been inspected in ranks and its inspection in quarters or camp is ordered, each man will arrange the prescribed articles on his bunk, if in quarters or permanent camp, or in front of his half of the tent, if in shelter tent camp, in the same relative order as shown in the illustrations accompanying this paragraph.

The captain, accompanied by the lieutenants, then inspects the quarters or camp. The first sergeant precedes the captain and calls the men to attention on entering each squad room or on approaching the tents; the men stand at attention but do not salute. (*C. I. D. R., No.* 16.)

**303.** If the inspection is to include an examination of the equipment while in ranks, the captain, after closing ranks, causes the company to stack arms, to march backward until 4 paces in rear of the stacks and to take intervals. He then commands: 1. *UNSLING EQUIPMENT.* 2. *OPEN PACKS.*

At the first command, each man unslings his equipment and places it on the ground at his feet, haversack to the front end of the pack 1 foot in front of toes.

At the second command, pack carriers are unstrapped, packs removed and unrolled, the longer edge of the pack along the lower edge of the cartridge belt. Each man exposes shelter tent pins, removes meat can, knife, fork, and spoon from the meat-can pouch, and places them on the right of the haversack, knife, fork, and spoon in the open meat can; removes the canteen and cup from the cover and places them on the left side of the haversack; unstraps and spreads out haversack so as to expose its contents; folds up the carrier to uncover the cartridge pockets; opens same; unrolls toilet articles and places them on the outer flap of the haversack; places underwear carried in pack on the left half of the open pack, with round fold parallel with front edge of pack; opens first-aid pouch and exposes contents to view. Special articles carried by individual men, such as flag kit, field glasses, compass, steel tape, notebook, etc., will be arranged on the right half of the open pack. Each man then resumes the attention.

The captain then passes along the ranks and file closers as before, inspects the equipment, returns to the right, and commands: *CLOSE PACKS*.

Each man rolls up his toilet articles and underwear, straps up his haversack and its contents, replaces the meat can, knife, fork, and spoon, and the canteen and cup; closes cartridge pockets and first-aid pouch; restores special articles to their proper receptacles; rolls up and replaces pack in carrier; and, leaving the equipment in its position on the ground, resumes the attention.

All equipments being packed, the captain commands: *SLING EQUIPMENT*.

The equipments are slung and belts fastened.

The captain then causes the company to assemble and take arms. The inspection is completed as already explained.

ARRANGEMENT OF EQUIPMENT FOR INSPECTION IN RANKS

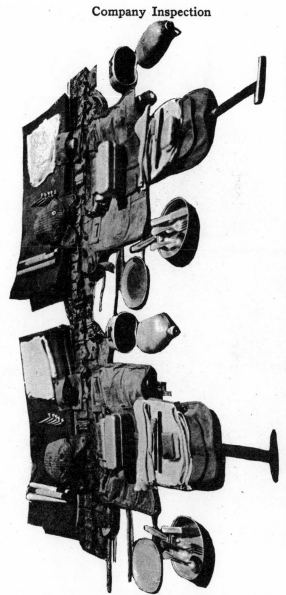

ARRANGEMENT OF EQUIPMENT FOR INSPECTION IN FRONT OF SHELTER TENT. FRONT OF TENT COMES ALONG FRONT EDGE OF BLANKETS

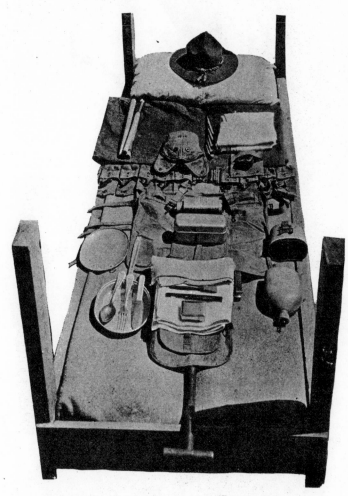

ARRANGEMENT OF EQUIPMENT ON BED FOR INSPECTION OF QUARTERS

FIG. 1

**304.** Method of "Inspecting a Rifle."

The command is: *PREPARE FOR INSPECTION.* **1.** The soldier brings his piece to the position of *INSPECTION ARMS.*

FIG. 2

2. The Inspector grasps the piece with the right hand, just below the lower band. (Fig. 1)

3. As soon as the Inspector touches the piece, the soldier drops his hands by his side to the "Position of the Soldier."

FIG. 3

4. The Inspector turns the muzzle to the left grasping the piece with the left hand at the balance, palm up; lets go with the right hand and regrasps the stock lightly near the heel with the thumb and fingers. (Fig. 3.) Examines the chamber, bolt and magazine mechanism.

5. The left hand is then slipped under the gun sling to a point just below the lower hand. Right hand retains grasp on stock, the rifle is turned over and the sling and under part of piece examined. (Fig. 4.)

FIG. 4

6. Retaining the grasp with the left hand under the gun sling, let go with the right hand, giving the stock a push, pivot the piece on the left hand; regrasp with the right hand near the muzzle and look through the barrel. (Fig. 5.)

FIG. 5

7. Again pivot the piece on the left hand, lowering the butt bringing it back to the position shown in (Fig. 3).

Let go with the right hand and again pivot the piece on the left, slipping the left hand on top and regrasping with the right, palm up, just above the balance (Fig. 6).

The piece is now in position to be handed back to the soldier.

FIG. 6

FIG. 7

8. The Inspector drops his left hand by his side, the soldier grasps the piece at the balance (just below the right hand of the Inspector). As soon as the soldier touches the piece the Inspector releases his hold with the right hand. (Fig. 7.)

9. The soldier closes the bolt, comes to the position of Port Arms and then to the position of Order Arms. (Fig. 8.)

FIG. 8

# CHAPTER VIII

## RATIONS—INDIVIDUAL COOKING

### The Ration

**305.** A ration is the allowance of food for one man for one day.

In the field there are three kinds of rations issued, as follows:

The *garrison ration* is intended to be issued in kind whenever possible. The approximate net weight of this ration is 4.5 pounds.

The *reserve ration* is the simplest efficient ration, and constitutes the reserve carried for field service. It consists of:

| | Ounces |
|---|---|
| Bacon | 12 |
| Hard bread | 16 |
| Coffee, roasted and ground | 1.12 |
| Sugar | 1.4 |
| Salt | .16 |
| Approximate net weight......pounds .... | 2 |

The *field ration* is the ration prescribed in orders by the commander of the field forces. It consists of the reserve ration, in whole or in part, supplemented by articles requisitioned or purchased locally or shipped from the rear.

In campaign a command carries as a part of its normal equipment the following rations:

(*a*) On each man: At least two days' reserve rations.

(*b*) In the ration section of the field train, for each man: Two days' field and one day's reserve rations.

(*c*) In the supply train: Two days' field rations.

In addition to the foregoing, commanders will require each man on the march to carry the unconsumed portion of the day's ration issued the night before for the noonday meal. Reserve rations are consumed only in case of extreme necessity, when other supplies are not available. They are not to be consumed or renewed without an express order from the officer in command of the troops who is responsible for the provision of supplies, namely, the division commander or other independent-detachment commander. Every officer within the limits of his command is held responsible for the enforcement of this regulation. Reserve rations consumed must be replaced at the first opportunity.

## Individual Cooking

**306.** Sometimes rations for several days are issued to the soldier at one time, and in such cases you should be very careful to so use the rations that they will last you the entire period. If you stuff yourself one day, or waste your rations, you will have to starve later on.

Generally the cooking for the company will be done by the company cook, but sometimes every soldier will have to prepare his own meals, using only his field mess kit for the purpose.

The best fire for individual cooking is a small, clear one, or, better yet, a few brisk coals. To make such a fire, first gather a number of sticks about 1 inch in diameter. These should be dry. Dead limbs adhering to a tree are dryer than those picked up from the ground. Split some of these and shave them up into kindling. Dig a trench in the ground, laid with the wind, about a foot long, 4 inches wide, and 6 inches deep. Start the fire in this trench gradually, piling on the heavier wood as the fire grows. When the trench is full of burning wood, allow it a few minutes to burn down to coals and stop blazing high. Then rest the meat can and cup over the trench and start cooking. Either may be supported, if necessary, with green sticks. If you cannot scrape a trench in the soil, build one up out of rocks or with two parallel logs.

The following recipes have been furnished from the office of the Quartermaster General, United States Army:

**307.** Coffee.—Fill the cup two-thirds full of cold water. Add one heaping spoonful of coffee and stir well, boil and then set it to the side of the fire to simmer for a few minutes. Add sugar. Then, to clear the coffee, throw in a spoonful or two of cold water. This coffee is of medium strength and is within the limit of the ration if made but twice a day.

**308.** *Cocoa.*—Take two-thirds of a cupful of water, bring to a boil, add one heaping spoonful of cocoa, and stir until dissolved. Add one spoonful of sugar, if desired, and boil for five minutes.

**309.** *Chocolate.*—Take two-thirds of a cupful of water, bring to a boil, add a piece of chocolate about the size of a hickory nut, breaking or cutting it into small pieces and stirring until dissolved. Add one spoonful of sugar, if desired, and boil for five minutes.

**310.** *Tea.*—Take two-thirds of a cupful of water, bring to a boil, add one-half of a level spoonful of tea, and then let it stand or "draw" for three minutes. If allowed to stand longer the tea will get bitter, unless separated from the tea leaves.

## Meats

**311.** *Bacon.*—Cut slices about five to the inch, three of which should generally be sufficient for one man for one meal. Place in a meat can with about one-half inch of cold water. Let come to a boil and then pour the water off. Fry over a brisk fire, turning the bacon once and quickly browning it. Remove the bacon to lid of meat can, leaving the grease for frying potatoes, onions, rice, flapjacks, etc., according to recipe.

**312.** Fresh meat (to fry).—To fry, a small amount of grease (one to two spoonfuls) is necessary. Put grease in the meat can and let come to a smoking temperature, then drop in the steak and, if about one-half inch thick, let fry for about one minute before turning, depending upon whether it is desired it shall be rare, medium, or well done. Then turn and fry briskly as before. Salt and pepper to taste.

Applies to beef, veal, pork, mutton, venison, etc.

**313.** *Fresh meat* (to broil).—Cut in slices about one inch thick, from half as large as the hand to four times that size. Sharpen a stick or branch of convenient length—say, from two to four feet long—and weave the point of the stick through the steak several times, so that it may be readily turned over a few brisk coals or on the windward side of a small fire. Allow to brown nicely, turning frequently. Salt and pepper to taste. Meat with considerable fat is preferred, though any meat may be broiled in this manner.

**314.** *Fresh meat* (to stew).—Cut into chunks from one-half inch to one inch cubes. Fill cup about one-third full of meat and cover with about one inch of water. Let boil or simmer about one hour, or until tender. Add such fibrous vegetables as carrots, turnips, or cabbage, cut into small chunks, soon after the meat is put on to boil, and potatoes, onions, or other tender vegetables when the meat is about half done. Amount of vegetables to be added, about the same as meat, depending upon supply and taste. Salt and pepper to taste. Applies to all fresh meats and fowls. The proportion of meat and vegetables used varies with their abundance, and fixed quantities can not be adhered to. Fresh fish can be handled as above, except that it is cooked much quicker, and potatoes and onions and canned corn are the only vegetables generally used with it, thus making a chowder. A slice of bacon would greatly improve the flavor. May be conveniently cooked in meat can or cup.

## Vegetables

**315.** *Potatoes* (fried).—Take two medium-size potatoes or one large one (about one-half pound), peel and cut into slices about one-fourth inch thick and scatter well in the meat can in which the grease remains after frying the bacon. Add sufficient water to half cover the potatoes, cover with the lid to keep the moisture in, and let come to a boil for about 15 to 20 minutes. Remove the cover and dry as desired. Salt and pepper to taste. During the cooking the bacon already prepared may be kept on the cover, which is most conveniently placed bottom side up over the cooking vegetables.

*Onions* (fried).—Same as potatoes.

**316.** *Potatoes* (boiled).—Peel two medium-sized potatoes (about one-half pound) or one large one, and cut in coarse chunks of about the same size—say 1½ inch cubes. Place in meat can and three-fourths fill with water. Cover with lid and let boil or simmer for 15 or 20 minutes. They are done when easily penetrated with a sharp stick. Pour off the water and let dry out for one or two minutes over hot ashes or light coals.

**317.** *Potatoes* (baked).—Take two medium-sized potatoes (about one-half pound) or one large one cut in half. Lay in a bed of light coals and cover with same and smother with ashes. Do not disturb for 30 or 40 minutes, when they should be done.

**318.** *Canned tomatoes.*—One 2-pound can is generally sufficient for five men.

**319.** *Stew.*—Pour into the meat can one man's allowance of tomatoes and add about two large hardtacks broken into small pieces and let come to a boil. Add salt and pepper to taste, or add a pinch of salt and one-fourth spoonful of sugar.

*Or,* having fried the bacon, pour the tomatoes into the meat can, the grease remaining, and add, if desired, two broken hardtacks. Set over a brisk fire and let come to a boil.

*Or,* heat the tomatoes just as they come from the can, adding two pinches of salt and one-half spoonful of sugar, if desired.

*Or,* especially in hot weather, eaten cold with hard bread they are very palatable.

**320.** *Rice.*—Take about two-thirds of a cupful of water, bring to a boil, add four heaping spoonfuls of rice, and boil until the grains are soft enough to be easily mashed between the fingers (about 20 minutes). Add two pinches of salt and, after stirring pour off the water and empty rice out on meat can. Bacon grease or sugar may be added.

**321.** *Corn meal, fine hominy, oatmeal.*—Take about one-third of a cupful of water, bring to a boil, add 4 heaping spoonfuls of the meal or hominy, and boil about 20 minutes. Then add about two pinches of salt and stir well.

**322.** *Dried beans and peas.*—Put 4 heaping spoonfuls in about two-thirds of a cupful of water and boil until soft. This generally takes from three to four hours. Add one pinch of salt. About half an hour before the beans are done add one slice of bacon.

## Hot Breads

**323.** *Flapjacks.*—Take 6 spoonfuls of flour and one-third spoonful of baking powder and mix thoroughly (or dry mix in a large pan before issue, at the rate of 25 pounds of flour and 3 half cans of baking powder for 100 men). Add sufficient cold water to make a batter that will drip freely from the spoon, adding a pinch of salt. Pour into the meat can, which should contain the grease from fried bacon or a spoonful of butter or fat, and place over medium hot coals sufficient to bake, so that in from 5 to 7 minutes the flapjack may be turned by a quick toss of the pan. Fry from 5 to 7 minutes longer, or until by examination it is found to be done.

**324.** *Hoecake.*—Hoecake is made exactly the same as flapjacks by substituting *corn meal* for *flour*.

**325.** *Emergency rations.*—Detailed instructions as to the manner of preparing the emergency ration are found on the label of each can. Remember that even a very limited amount of bacon or hard bread, or both, consumed with the emergency ration makes it far more palatable, and generally extends the period during which it can be consumed with relish. For this reason it would be better to husband the supply of hard bread and bacon for use with the emergency ration when it becomes evident that the latter must be consumed rather than to retain the emergency ration to the last extremity and force its exclusive use for a longer period than two or three days.

# CHAPTER IX

## MILITARY DISCIPLINE AND COURTESY

### Obedience

**326.** The very first paragraph in the Army Regulations reads:

"All persons in the military service are required to *obey strictly* and to *execute promptly* the lawful orders of their superiors."

Obedience is the first and last duty of a soldier. It is the foundation upon which all military efficiency is built. Without it an army becomes a mob, while with it a mob ceases to be a mob and becomes possessed of much of the power of an organized force. It is a quality that is demanded of every person in the Army, from the highest to the lowest. Each enlisted man binds himself, by his enlistment oath, to obedience. Each officer, in accepting his commission, must take upon himself the same solemn obligation.

Obey strictly and execute promptly the lawful orders of your superiors. It is enough to know that the person giving the order, whether he be an officer, a noncommissioned officer, or a private acting as such, is your lawful superior. You may not like him, you may not respect him, but you must respect his position and authority, and reflect honor and credit upon yourself and your profession by yielding to all superiors that complete and unhesitating obedience which is the pleasure as well as the duty of every true soldier.

Orders must be *strictly* carried out. It is not sufficient to comply with only that part which suits you or which involves no work or danger or hardship. Nor is it proper or permissible, when you are ordered to do a thing in a certain way or to accomplish a work in a definitely prescribed manner, for you to obtain the same results by other methods.

Obedience must be *prompt and unquestioning*. When any soldier (and this word includes officers as well as enlisted men) receives an order, it is not for him to consider whether the order is a good one or not, whether it would have been better had such an order never been given, or whether the duty might be better performed by some one else, or at some other time, or in some other manner. His duty is, first, to understand just what the order requires, and, second, to proceed at once to carry out the order to the best of his ability.

"Officers and men of all ranks and grades are given a certain independence in the execution of the tasks to which they are assigned and are expected to show initiative in meeting the different situations as they arise. Every individual, from the highest commander to the lowest private, must always remember that inaction and neglect of opportunities will warrant more severe censure than an error in the choice of the means."
—(*Preface, Field Service Regulations.*)

### Loyalty

**327.** But even with implicit obedience you may yet fail to measure up to that high standard of duty which is at once the pride and glory of every true soldier. Not until you carry out the desires and wishes of your superiors in a hearty, willing, and cheerful manner are you meeting all the requirements of your profession. For an order is but the will of your superior, however it may be expressed. Loyalty means that you are for your organization and its officers and noncommissioned officers—not against them; that you always extend your most earnest and hearty support to those in authority. No soldier is a loyal soldier who is a knocker or a grumbler or a shirker. Just one man of this class in a company breeds discontent and dissatisfaction among many others. You should, therefore, not only guard against doing such things yourself but should discourage such actions among any of your comrades.

### Discipline

**328.** "1. All persons in the military service are required to obey strictly and to execute promptly the lawful orders of their superiors.

"2. Military authority will be exercised with firmness, kindness, and justice. Punishments must conform to law and follow offenses as promptly as circumstances will permit.

"3. Superiors are forbidden to injure those under their authority by tyrannical or capricious conduct or by abusive language. While maintaining discipline and the thorough and prompt performance of military duty, all officers, in dealing with enlisted men, will bear in mind the absolute necessity of so treating them as to preserve their self-respect. Officers will keep in as close touch as possible with the men under their command and will strive to build up such relations of confidence and sympathy as will insure the free approach of their men to them for counsel and assistance. This relationship may be gained and maintained without relaxation of the bonds of discipline and with great benefit to the service as a whole.

"4. Courtesy among military men is indispensable to discipline; respect to superiors will not be confined to obedience on duty, but will be extended on all occasions.

"5. Deliberations or discussions among military men conveying praise or censure, or any mark of approbation, toward others in the military service, and all publications relating to private or personal transactions between officers are prohibited. Efforts to influence legislation affecting the Army or to procure personal favor or consideration should never be made except through regular military channels; the adoption of any other method by any officer or enlisted man will be noted in the military record of those concerned." (*Army Regulations.*)

**329.** The discipline which makes the soldier of a free country reliable in battle is not to be gained by harsh or tyrannical treatment. On the contrary, such treatment is far more likely to destroy than to make an army. It is possible to impart instruction and give commands in such manner and in such tone of voice as to inspire in the soldier no feeling but an intense desire to obey, while the opposite manner and tone of voice can not fail to excite strong resentment and a desire to disobey. The one mode or the other of dealing with subordinates springs from a corresponding spirit in the breast of the commander. He who feels the respect which is due to others can not fail to inspire in them regard for himself, while he who feels, and hence manifests, disrespect toward others, especially his inferiors, can not fail to inspire hatred against himself." (*Address of Maj. Gen. John M. Schofield to the United States Corps of Cadets, Aug. 11, 1879.*)

**330.** When, by long-continued drill and subordination, you have learned your duties, and obedience becomes second nature, you have acquired discipline. It can not be acquired in a day nor a month. It is a growth. It is the habit of obedience. To teach this habit of obedience is the main object of the close-order drill, and, if good results are to be expected, the greatest attention must be paid to even the smallest details. The company or squad must be formed promptly at the prescribed time—not a minute or even a second late. All must wear the exact uniform prescribed and in the exact manner prescribed. When at attention there must be no gazing about, no raising of hands, no chewing or spitting in ranks. The manual of arms and all movements must be executed absolutely as prescribed. A drill of this kind teaches discipline. A careless, sloppy drill breeds disobedience and insubordination. In other words, discipline simply means *efficiency*.

## Military Courtesy

**331.** In all walks of life men who are gentlemanly and of good breeding are always respectful and courteous to those about them. It helps to make life move along more smoothly. In civil life this courtesy is shown by the custom of tipping the hat to ladies, shaking hands with friends, and greeting persons with a nod or a friendly "Good morning," etc.

In the Army courtesy is just as necessary, and for the same reasons. It helps to keep the great machine moving without friction.

**332.** "Courtesy among military men is indispensable to discipline; respect to superiors will not be confined to obedience on duty, but will be extended on all occasions." (*Par. 4, Army Regulations,* 1913.)

**333.** One method of extending this courtesy is by saluting. When in ranks the question of what a private should do is simple—he obeys any command that is given. It is when out of ranks that a private must know how and when to salute.

## Saluting

**334.** In the old days the free men of Europe were all allowed to carry weapons, and when they met each would hold up his right hand to show that he had no weapon in it and that they met as friends. Slaves or serfs, however, were not allowed to carry weapons, and slunk past the free men without making any sign. In this way the salute came to be the symbol or sign by which soldiers (free men) might recognize each other. The lower classes began to imitate the soldiers in this respect, although in a clumsy, apologetic way, and thence crept into civil life the custom of raising the hand or nodding as one passed an acquaintance. The soldiers, however, kept their individual salute, and purposely made it intricate and difficult to learn in order that it could be acquired only by the constant training all real soldiers received. To this day armies have preserved their salute, and when correctly done it is at once recognized and never mistaken for that of the civilian. All soldiers should be careful to execute the salute exactly as prescribed. The civilian or the imitation soldier who tries to imitate the military salute, invariably makes some mistake which shows that he is not a real soldier; he gives it in an apologetic manner, he fails to stand or march at attention, his coat is unbuttoned or hat on awry, or he fails to look the person saluted in the eye. There is a wide difference in the method of rendering and meaning between the civilian salute as used by friends in passing, or by servants to their employers, and the MILITARY SALUTE, the symbol and sign of the military profession.

**335.** *To salute with the hand,* first assume the position of a soldier or march at attention. Look the officer you are to salute straight in the eye. Then, when the proper distance separates you, raise the right hand smartly till the tip of the forefinger touches the lower part of the headdress or forehead above the right eye, thumb and fingers extended and joined, palm to the left, forearm inclined at about 45°, hand and wrist straight. Continue to look the officer you are saluting straight in the eye and keep your hand in the position of salute until the officer acknowledges the salute or until he has passed. Then drop the hand smartly to the side. The salute is given with the right hand only.

**336.** *To salute with the rifle,* bring the rifle to right shoulder arms if not already there. Carry the left hand smartly to the small of the stock, forearm horizontal, palm of the hand down, thumb and fingers extended and joined, forefinger touching the end of the cocking piece. Look the officer saluted in the eye. When the officer has acknowledged the salute or has passed, drop the left hand smartly to the side and turn the head and eyes to the front. The rifle salute may also be executed from the order or trail.

**337.** *To salute with the saber,* bring the saber to order saber if not already there, raise and carry the saber to the front, base of the hilt as high as the chin and 6 inches in front of the neck, edge to the left, point 6 inches farther to the front than the hilt, thumb extended on the left of the grip, all fingers grasping the grip. Look the officer saluted in the eye. When the officer has acknowledged the salute or has passed, lower the saber, point in prolongation of the right foot and near the ground, edge to the left, hand by the side, thumb on left of grip, arm extended, and return to the order saber. If mounted, the hand is held behind the thigh, point a little to the right and front of the stirrup.

The *pistol* is not carried in the hand but in the holster, therefore when armed with the pistol salute with the hand.

Always stand or march at attention before and during the salute. The hat should be on straight, coat completely buttoned up, and hands out of the pockets.

## Rules Governing Saluting

**338.** (1) Salutes shall be exchanged between officers and enlisted men not in a military formation, nor at drill, work, games, or mess, on every occasion of their meeting, passing near or being addressed, the officer junior in rank or the enlisted man saluting first.

(2) When an officer enters a room where there are several enlisted men the word "attention" is given by some one who perceives him, when all rise, uncover, and remain standing at attention until the officer leaves the room or directs otherwise. Enlisted men at meals stop eating and remain seated at attention.

(3) An enlisted man, if seated, rises on the approach of an officer, faces toward him, stands at attention, and salutes. Standing, he faces an officer for the same purpose. If the parties remain in the same place or on the same ground, such compliments need not be repeated. Soldiers actually at work do not cease work to salute an officer unless addressed by him.

(4) Before addressing an officer an enlisted man makes the prescribed salute with the weapon with which he is armed, or, if unarmed, with the right hand. He also makes the same salute after receiving a reply.

(5) In uniform, covered or uncovered, but not in formation, officers and enlisted men salute military persons as follows: With arms in hand, the salute prescribed for that arm (sentinels on interior guard duty excepted) ; without arms, the right-hand salute.

(6) In civilian dress, covered or uncovered, officers and enlisted men salute military persons with the right-hand salute.

(7) Officers and enlisted men will render the prescribed salute in a military manner, the officer junior in rank or the enlisted men saluting first. When several officers in company are saluted all entitled to the salute shall return it.

(8) Except in the field under campaign or simulated campaign conditions, a mounted officer (or soldier) dismounts before addressing a superior officer not mounted.

(9) A man in formation shall not salute when directly addressed, but shall come to attention if at rest or at ease.

(10) Saluting distance is that within which recognition is easy. In general, it does not exceed 30 paces.

(11) When an officer entitled to the salute passes in rear of a body of troops, it is brought to attention while he is opposite the post of the commander.

(12) In public conveyances, such as railway trains and street cars, and in public places, such as theatres, honors and personal salutes may be omitted when palpably inappropriate or apt to disturb or annoy civilians present.

(13) Soldiers at all times and in all situations pay the same compliments to officers of the Army, Navy, Marine Corps, and Volunteers, and to officers of the National Guard as to officers of their own regiment, corps, or arm of service.

(14) Sentinels on post doing interior guard duty conform to the foregoing principles, but salute by presenting arms when armed with the rifle. They will not salute if it interferes with the proper performance of their duties. Troops under arms will salute as prescribed in drill regulations.

**339.** (1) Commanders of detachments or other commands will salute officers of grades higher than the person commanding the unit, by first bringing the unit to attention and then saluting as required by subparagraph (5), paragraph 759. If the person saluted is of a junior or equal grade, the unit need not be at attention in the exchange of salutes.

(2) If two detachments or other commands meet, their commanders will exchange salutes, both commands being at attention.

Salutes and honors as a rule, are not paid by troops actually engaged in drill, on the march, or in the field under campaign or simulated campaign conditions. Troops on the service of security pay no compliments whatever.

**340.** If the command is in line at a halt (not in the field), and armed with the rifle, or with sabers drawn, it shall be brought to *present arms* or *present sabers* before its commander salutes in the following cases: When the National Anthem is played, or when to *the color* or to *the standard* is sounded during ceremonies, or when a person is saluted who is its immediate or higher commander or a general officer, or when the national or regimental color is saluted.

**341.** At parades and other ceremonies, under arms, the command shall render the prescribed salute and shall remain in the position of salute while the National Anthem is being played; also at retreat and during ceremonies when to *the color* is played, if no band is present. If not under arms, the organizations shall be brought to attention at the first note of the National Anthem, *to the color* or *to the standard,* and the salute rendered by the officer or noncommissioned officer in command as prescribed in regulations, as amended herein.

**342.** Whenever the National Anthem is played at any place when persons belonging to the military service are present, all officers and enlisted men not in formation shall stand at attention facing toward the music (except at retreat, when they shall face toward the flag). If in uniform, covered or uncovered, or in civilian clothes, uncovered, they shall salute at the first note of the anthem, retaining the position of salute until the last note of the anthem. If not in uniform and covered, they shall uncover at the first note of the anthem, holding the headdress opposite the left shoulder and so remain until its close, except that in inclement weather the headdress may be slightly raised.

The same rules apply when *to the color* or *to the standard* is sounded as when the National Anthem is played.

When played by an Army band, the National Anthem shall be played through without repetition of any part not required to be repeated to make it complete.

The same marks of respect prescribed for observance during the playing of the National Anthem of the United States shall be shown toward the national anthem of any other country when played upon official occasions.

**343.** Officers and enlisted men passing the unopened color will render honors as follows: If in uniform, they will salute as required by subparagraph (5), paragraph 338; if in civilian dress and covered, they will uncover, holding the headdress opposite the left shoulder with the right hand; if uncovered, they will salute with the right-hand salute."

The national flag belonging to dismounted organizations is called a color; to mounted organizations, a standard. An uncased color is one that is not in its waterproof cover.

Privates do not salute noncommissioned officers. *Prisoners are not permitted to salute;* they merely come to attention if not actually at work. The playing of the National Anthem as a part of a medley is prohibited in the military service.

## Courtesies in Conversation

**344.** In speaking to an officer, always stand at attention and use the word "Sir." Examples:

"Sir, Private Brown, Company B, reports as orderly."

"Sir, the first sergeant directed me to report to the captain."

(Question by an officer:) "To what company do you belong?"

(Answer:) "Company H, sir."

(Question by an officer:) "Has first call for drill sounded?"

(Answer:) "Yes, sir; it sounded about five minutes ago."

(Question by a Captain:) "Can you tell me, please, where Major Smith's tent is?"

(Answer:) "Yes, sir; I'll take the Captain to it."

Use the third person in speaking to an officer. Examples: "Does the Lieutenant wish," etc.

"Did the Captain send for Sergeant Brown?"

In delivering a message from one officer to another, always use the form similar to the following: "Lieutenant A presents his compliments to Captain B and states," etc. This form is not used when the person sending or receiving the message is an enlisted man.

In all official conversation refer to other soldiers by their titles, thus: Sergeant B, Private C.

# CHAPTER X

## UNIFORM AND EQUIPMENT

**345.** FIELD UNIFORM AND INDIVIDUAL EQUIPMENT FOR ALL ENLISTED MEN

| Orders | Articles | How Carried | Remarks |
|---|---|---|---|
| **(A) FIELD UNIFORM** | | | |
| Page 62 U. R. 1914 and Table XXVI G. O. 39 1915 | 1 Hat, service, with tying cord, hat cord sewed on, hat peaked 4 indentations ............. <br> 1 shirt, flannel, O. D........ <br> 1 shoes, marching, prs........ <br> 1 Leggins and laces, prs...... <br> 1 Breeches, service, O. D..... <br> 1 Identification tag and tape.. <br> 1 Waist belt, web, O. D...... <br> 1 Drawers, prs............... <br> 1 Stockings, woolen, prs...... <br> 1 Undershirt ............... | To be worn <br><br> Worn around neck under shirt | Par. 77 U. R. <br><br> Chevrons sewed on |
| **(B) FIELD EQUIPMENT** | | | |
| Table 14 (d) <br><br> IUAEM | 1 First Aid pkt. and pouch.... <br> 1 Haversack ................ <br> 1 Can Bacon ................ <br> 1 Can, condiment ........... <br> 1 Canteen, with cover ...... <br> 1 Cup ...................... <br> 1 Meat can ................. <br> 1 Knife .................... <br> 1 Fork ..................... <br> 1 Spoon ................... | Worn behind seam of breeches left of Belt fastener <br><br> Worn on right buttock <br> Carried in haversack pouch | Change O.U.R. No. 19, 1917, to U. R. 74 <br><br><br> U. R. 63 <br><br> U. R. 88 |
| **(C) SERVICE KIT** | | | |
| G. O. No. 56 1915 <br><br> G. O. No. 39, 1915 <br><br> Par. 302 FSR Table XXVI G. O. 39, 1915 | Field Kit (clothing component, in addition to that worn on person) <br> 1 Blanket, O. D............. <br> 1 Comb .................... <br> 1 Drawers, prs.............. <br> 1 Poncho .................. <br> 1 Soap, cake ............... <br> 1 Shoestrings, prs........... <br> 2 Stockings, woolen ......... <br> 1 Toothbrush .............. <br> 1 Towel ................... <br> 1 Undershirt ............... <br> 5 Pins, tent, shelter......... <br> 1 Tent, shelter, half, dismounted <br> 2 Rations, reserve .......... <br> 1 Head net, mosquito ....... <br> 1 Bar, mosquito ............ | Rolled into a pack in pack carrier <br><br><br><br> In haversack <br> When ordered <br> For two men | |

ADDITIONAL EQUIPMENT FOR SUPPLY SGTS., MESS SGTS., SGTS., CPLS.,
COOKS, MECH., PRTS., 1ST CL. AND PRTS.

| Orders | Articles | How Carried | Remarks |
|---|---|---|---|
| IUAEM<br>Table<br>14 (d) | 1 United States rifle, cal. 30<br>1 Oiler and thong case, with<br>    brush and thong or 1<br>    spare part container....<br>1 Gun sling ...............<br>1 Front sight cover ........<br>1 Cartridge belt ...........<br>100 Cartridges ball, cal. 30.... | In butt of rifle,<br>oiler filled,<br>thong<br>full length | |

ADDITIONAL FOR ALL SGTS.

| | | | |
|---|---|---|---|
| IUAEM<br>Table 1<br>Table 2<br>XXVI<br>G. O. 39<br>1915 | 1 Compass, watch .........<br>1 Field glass, Type E. E. (2 per Co.)<br>1 Note book ...............<br>1 Pencil ..................<br>1 Field message book.......<br>1 Whistle and chain (Acme<br>    Thunderer) ............ | | |

ADDITIONAL FOR CPLS. AND SQUAD LEADERS

| | | | |
|---|---|---|---|
| XXVI<br>G. O. 39<br>1915<br>and<br>IUAEM<br>Table<br>14 (m) | 1 Note book ...............<br>1 Pencil ...................<br>1 Housewife and contents—<br>    AR 1215, Par. 11.......<br>1 Cleaning rod and case .....<br>4 Drift Slides ..............<br>1 Screw driver .............<br>1 Foot powder, can ........<br>1 Adhesive tape, roll ....... | | |

ADDITIONAL FOR 1ST SGTS., AND BUGLERS

| | | | |
|---|---|---|---|
| IUEAM<br>Table 14 (e) | 1 Pistol ...................<br>1 Pistol holster ............<br>1 Pistol belt, without saber ring<br>1 Magazine pocket .........<br>2 Magazines, extra ........<br>21 Cartridges, pistol ........ | Worn on right<br>side, outside<br>overcoat,<br>when worn | |

ADDITIONAL FOR 1ST SGTS.

| | | | |
|---|---|---|---|
| IUEAM<br>Table 14 (e)<br>Table 2 | 1 Steel tape, 5 ft............<br>1 Field glass, type EE....... | | |

ADDITIONAL FOR BUGLERS

| | | | |
|---|---|---|---|
| IUEAM<br>Table 2<br>Table 14 (f)<br>Table 2<br>Table 14 (e)<br>G. O. 39<br>W. D.<br>1915 | 1 Wire cutter ..............<br>1 Wire cutter carrier .......<br>1 Kit flag, combination In-<br>    fantry ................<br>1 Field glass (Type A or B)<br>1 Bugle and sling .........<br>1 Whistle, Kinglet ......... | | |

INTRENCHING TOOLS—For each squad of a company

| | | | |
|---|---|---|---|
| IUAEM<br>Table<br>14 (n) | 4 Shovels and carriers ......<br>2 Pick mattocks and carriers.<br>1 Wire cutter and carrier ...<br>For each odd numbered squad<br>1 Bolo and scabbard ........<br>For each even numbered squad<br>1 Hand axe and carrier..... | Nos. 1 and 3 F.R. 2 & 4 R.R.<br>No. 2 F. R., 1 R. R.<br>Squad leader.<br><br>No. 3 R. R.<br><br>No. 3 R. R. | |

## Uniforms

**346.** Uniforms and clothing issued to enlisted men must not be sold, pawned, loaned, given away, lost or damaged through neglect or carelessness. Any soldier who violates this rule may be tried by a military court and punished.

All uniforms and articles of clothing issued to enlisted men, whether or not charged on their clothing allowance, remain the property of the United States and do not become the property of the soldier either before or after discharge from the service. Under the law a soldier honorably discharged from the Army of the United States is authorized to wear his uniform from the place of his discharge to his home within three months after the date of such discharge. To wear the uniform after three months from the date of such discharge renders such person liable to fine or imprisonment, or both.

The *dress uniform* (the blue uniform) consists of the dress cap, dress coat, dress trousers, and russet-leather shoes. The straight, standing, military, white linen collar, showing no opening in front, is always worn with this uniform, with not to exceed one-half inch showing above the collar of the coat. Turndown, piccadilly, or roll collars are not authorized.

When under arms, white gloves and the garrison belt (or russet-leather belt and cartridge box) are worn.

The *full-dress uniform* is the same as the dress uniform, with the breast cord added.

The *service uniform* is either cotton (summer) or woolen (winter) olive drab.

For duty in the field it consists of the service hat, with cord sewed on, service coat or sweater, service breeches, olive-drab flannel shirt, leggings, russet-leather shoes, and identification tag. In cold weather olive-drab woolen gloves are worn; at other times, no gloves.

When not in the field, the service cap is worn instead of the campaign hat. Under arms, white gloves and the garrison belt (or russet-leather belt and cartridge box) are worn.

Wear the exact uniform prescribed by your commanding officer, whether you are on duty or off duty.

Never wear a mixed uniform, as, for instance, a part of the service uniform with the blue uniform.

Never wear any part of the uniform with civilian clothes. It is very unsoldierly, for example, to wear a civilian overcoat over the uniform or to wear the uniform overcoat over a civilian suit.

Keep the uniform clean and neat and in good repair.

Grease spots and dust and dirt should be removed as soon as possible.

Rips and tears should be promptly mended.

Missing buttons and cap and collar ornaments should be promptly replaced.

There is but one correct and soldierly way to wear the cap. Never wear it on the back or side of the head.

The service mat should be worn in the regulation shape, peaked, with four indentations, and with hat cord sewed on. Do not cover it with pen or pencil marks.

Never appear outside your room or tent with your coat or olive-drab shirt unbuttoned or collar of coat unhooked. Chevrons, service stripes, and campaign medals and badges are a part of the uniform and must be worn as prescribed.

When coats are not worn with the service uniform olive-drab shirts are prescribed.

Suspenders must never be worn exposed to view.

Never appear in breeches without leggings.

Leather leggings should be kept polished. Canvas leggings should be scrubbed when dirty.

Russet-leather (tan) shoes should be kept clean and polished.

The overcoat when worn must be buttoned throughout and the collar hooked. When the belt is worn it will be worn outside the overcoat.

# CHAPTER XI

## LAWS AND REGULATIONS

### GENERAL PROVISIONS

**347.** The Army of the United States is governed by certain laws called "The Articles of War" and certain regulations called "Army Regulations."

The following list includes the offenses most often committed by soldiers, generally through ignorance or carelessness rather than viciousness. Violation of any rule or regulation should be carefully guarded against, since they not only subject the offender to punishment, but also bring discredit on his comrades, his organization, and on the military profession:

1. Selling, pawning, or, through neglect, losing or spoiling any Government property, such as uniforms, blankets, equipment, ammunition, etc.

2. Disobedience of the orders of any officer or noncommissioned officer.

3. Disrespect to an officer or noncommissioned officer.

4. Absence from camp without leave.

5. Absence from any drill, formation, or other duty without authority.

6. Drunkenness on duty or off duty, whether in camp or when absent either with or without leave.

7. Bringing liquor into camp.

8. Noisy or disorderly conduct in camp or when absent either with or without leave.

9. Entering on private property, generally for the purpose of stealing fruit, etc.

10. Negligence or carelessness at drill or on other duty, particularly while on guard or as a sentinel over prisoners.

11. Wearing an unauthorized uniform or wearing the uniform in an improper manner.

12. Urinating in or around camp.

13. Failing to salute properly.

14. Disrespect or affront to a sentinel.

15. Abuse or neglect of his horse.

"The basic principles of the combat tactics of the different arms are set forth in the Drill Regulations of those arms for units as high as brigades." (*Preface, Field Service Regulations.*)

"The Drill Regulations are furnished as a guide. They provide the principles for training and for increasing the probability of success in battle. In the interpretation of the regulations the spirit must be sought. Quibbling over the minutiæ of form is indicative of failure to grasp the spirit." (*Paragraph 4, Infantry Drill Regulations.*)

Field Service Regulations govern all arms of the Army of the United States.

## The Army of the United States

**348**. The Army of the United States shall consist of the Regular Army, the Volunteer Army, the Officers' Reserve Corps, the Enlisted Reserve Corps, the National Guard while in the service of the United States, and such other land forces as are now or may hereafter be authorized by law. (Sec. 1, act of June 3, 1916.)

## Rank and precedence of officers and noncommissioned officers

**349**. The following are the grades of rank of officers and noncommissioned officers:

| Army | Navy |
|------|------|
| 7. Captain. | Vice Admiral. |
| 6. Major. | Rear Admiral. |
| 8. First lieutenant. | Captain. |
| 5. Lieutenant colonel. | Commander. |
| 4. Colonel. | Lieut. Commander. |
| 3. Brigadier general. | Lieutenant. |
| 2. Major general. | Lieut., Junior grade. |
| 1. Lieutenant general. | Ensign. |
| 9. Second lieutenant. | |
| 10. Aviator, Signal Corps. | |
| 11. Cadet. | |

12. (*a*) Sergeant major, regimental; sergeant major, senior grade, Coast Artillery Corps; (*b*) quartermaster sergeant, senior grade, Quartermaster Corps; master hospital sergeant, Medical Department; master engineer, senior grade, Corps of Engineers; master electrician, Coast Artillery Corps; master signal electrician; band leader; (*c*) hospital sergeant, Medical Department; master engineer, junior grade, Corps of Engineers; engineer, Coast Artillery Corps.

13. Ordnance sergeant; quartermaster sergeant, Quartermaster Corps; supply sergeant, regimental.

14. Sergeant major, squadron and battalion; sergeant major, junior grade, Coast Artillery Corps; supply sergeant, battalion, Corps of Engineers.

15. (*a*) First sergeant; (*b*) sergeant, first class, Medical Department; sergeant, first class, Quartermaster Corps; sergeant, first class, Corps of Engineers; sergeant, first class, Signal Corps; electrician sergeant, first class, Coast Artillery Corps; electrician sergeant, Artillery Detachment, United States Military Academy; assistant engineer, Coast Artillery Corps; (*c*) master gunner, Coast Artillery Corps; master gunner, Artillery Detachment, United States Military Academy; band sergeant and assistant leader, United States Military Academy band; assistant band leader; sergeant bugler; electrician sergeant, second class, Coast Artillery Corps; electrician sergeant, second class, Artillery Detachment, United States Military Academy; radio sergeant.

16. Color sergeant.

17. Sergeant; supply sergeant, company; mess sergeant; stable sergeant; fireman, Coast Artillery Corps.

18. Corporal.

In each grade and subgrade date of commission, appointment, or warrant determines the order of precedence. (*Paragraph 9, Army Regulations, 1913.*)

## Insignia of Officers and Noncommissioned Officers

**350.** The insignia of rank appearing on the shoulder straps, shoulder loops, or collar of shirt (when shirt is worn without coat) of officers are as follows:

General: Coat of arms and two stars.

Lieutenant general: One large star and two smaller ones.

Major general: Two silver stars.

Brigadier general: One silver star.

Colonel: One silver spread eagle.

Lieutenant colonel: One silver leaf.

Major: One gold leaf.

Captain: Two silver bars.

First lieutenant. One silver bar.

The grade of noncommissioned officers is indicated by chevrons worn on the sleeve.

## Extracts from the Articles of War
### (Relating to enlisted men.)
### Certain Articles To Be Read and Explained

**351.** ART. 110. Articles 1, 2, and 29, 54 to 96 inclusive, and 104 to 109, inclusive, shall be read and explained to every soldier at the time of his enlistment or muster in, or within six days thereafter, and shall be read and explained once every six months to the soldiers of every garrison, regiment, or company in the service of the United States.

## Definitions

**352.** ARTICLE 1. The following words when used in these articles shall be construed in the sense indicated in this article, unless the context shows that a different sense is intended, namely:

(*a*) The word "officer" shall be construed to refer to a commissioned officer;

(*b*) The word "soldier" shall be construed as including a noncommissioned officer, a private, or any other enlisted man;

(*c*) The word "company" shall be understood as including a troop or battery; and

(*d*) The word "battalion" shall be understood as including a squadron.

## Persons Subject to Military Law

**353.** ART. 2. The following persons are subject to these articles and shall be understood as included in the term "any person subject to military law" or "persons subject to military law" whenever used in these articles: *Provided,* That nothing contained in this act, except as specifically provided in article 2, subparagraph (*c*), shall be construed to apply to any person under the United States naval jurisdiction, unless otherwise specifically provided by law:

(*a*) All officers and soldiers belonging to the Regular Army of the United States; all volunteers, from the dates of their muster or acceptance into the military service of the United States; and all other persons lawfully called, drafted, or ordered into or to duty or for training in the said service, from the dates they are required by the terms of the call, draft, or order to obey the same.

(*b*) Cadets.

(*c*) Officers and soldiers of the Marine Corps when detached for service with the armies of the United States by order of the President: *Provided,* That an officer or soldier of the Marine Corps when so detached may be tried by military court-martial for an offense committed against the laws for the government of the naval service prior to his detachment, and for an offense committed against these articles he may be tried by a naval court-martial after such detachment ceases.

(*d*) All retainers to the camp and all persons accompanying or serving with the armies of the United States without the territorial jurisdiction of the United States, and in time of war all such retainers and persons accompanying or serving with the armies of the United States in the field, both within and without the territorial jurisdiction of the United States, though not otherwise subject to these articles.

(e) All persons under sentence adjudged by courts-martial.

(f) All persons admitted into the Regular Army Soldiers' Home at Washington, D. C.

## Enlistment Without Discharge

**354. Art. 29.** Any soldier who, without having first received a regular discharge again enlists in the Army, or in the militia when in the service of the United States, or in the Navy or Marine Corps of the United States, or in any foreign army, shall be deemed to have deserted the service of the United States; and, where enlistment is in one of the forces of the United States mentioned above, to have fraudulently enlisted therein.

## Fraudulent Enlistment

**355. Art. 54.** Any person who shall procure himself to be enlisted in the military service of the United States by means of wilful misrepresentation or concealment as to his qualifications for enlistment, and shall receive pay or allowances under such enlistment, shall be punished as a court-martial may direct.

### Penalty:

Enlistment, fraudulent:

Procured by means of willful misrepresentation or concealment of a fact in regard to a prior enlistment or discharge, or in regard to a conviction of a civil or military offense, or in regard to imprisonment under sentence of a court. D. D.; 1 yr.

## Officer Making Unlawful Enlistment

**356. Art. 55.** Any officer who knowingly enlists or musters into the military service any person whose enlistment or muster in is prohibited by law, regulations, or orders shall be dismissed from the service or suffer such other punishment as a court-martial may direct.

## Muster Rolls—False Muster

**357. Art. 56.** At every muster of a regiment, troop, battery, or company the commanding officer thereof shall give to the mustering officer certificates, signed by himself, stating how long absent officers have been absent and the reasons of their absence. And the commanding officer of every troop, battery, or company shall give like certificates, stating how long absent noncommissioned officers and private soldiers have been absent and the reasons of their absence. Such reasons and time of absence shall be inserted in the muster rolls opposite the names of the respective absent officers and soldiers, and the certificates, together with the muster rolls, shall be transmitted by the mustering officer to the Department of War as speedily as the distance of the place and muster will admit. Any officer who knowingly makes a false muster of man or animal, or who signs or directs or allows the signing of any muster roll knowing the same to contain false muster or false statement as to the absence or pay of an officer or soldier, or who wrongfully takes money or other consideration on mustering in a regiment, company, or other organization, or on signing muster rolls, or who knowingly musters as an officer or soldier a person who is not such officer or soldier, shall be dismissed from the service and suffer such other punishment as a court-martial may direct.

### False Returns—Omission to Render Returns

**358.** ART. 57. Every officer commanding a regiment, an independent troop, battery, or company, or a garrison shall, in the beginning of every month, transmit, through the proper channels, to the War Department an exact return of the same, specifying the names of the officers then absent from their posts, with the reasons for and the time of their absence. Every officer whose duty it is to render to the War Department or other superior authority a return of the state of the troops under his command, or of the arms, ammunition, clothing, funds, or other property thereonto belonging, who knowingly makes a false return thereof shall be dismissed from the service and suffer such other punishment as a court-martial may direct. And any officer who, through neglect or design, omits to render such return shall be punished as a court-martial may direct.

### Desertion

**359.** ART. 58. Any person subject to military law who deserts or attempts to desert the service of the United States

D. D.=Dishonorable Discharge, forfeiture of all pay and allowances due and to become due.

C.=Confinement at hard labor; example: C—6 mo., means confinement at hard labor for a period of six months.

F⅔=3 mo.=Forfeiture of ⅔ of pay for three months; or —— days= Forfeiture of pay for so many days.

Penalty:

Attempting to desert:
  After not more than six months in service.  D. D.; C—6 mo.
  After more than six months in service.  D. D.; C.—1 yr.
  In the execution of a conspiracy or in the presence of an unlawful
    assemblage which the troops may be opposing.  D. D.; C.—3 yrs.
Desertion:
  Terminated by apprehension:
    Not more than 6 months in service at time of desertion.  D. D.;
      C.—1½ yrs.
    More than 6 months in service at time of desertion.  D. D.;
      C.—2½ yrs.
  Terminated by surrender:
    After absence of not more than 30 days.  D. D.; C.—1 yr.
    After absence of more than 30 days.  D. D.; C.—1½ yrs.
  In the execution of a conspiracy or in the presence of an unlawful
    assemblage which the troops may be opposing.  D. D.; C.—5 yrs.

shall, if the offense be committed in time of war, suffer death
or such other punishment as a court-martial may direct, and,
if the offense be committed at any other time, any punishment,
excepting death, that a court-martial may direct.

## Advising or Aiding Another to Desert

360.  ART. 59.  Any person subject to military law who advises or persuades or knowingly assists another to desert the
service of the United States shall, if the offense be committed
in time of war, suffer death or such other punishment as a
court-martial may direct, and if the offense be committed at
any other time any punishment, excepting death, that a court-
martial may direct.

Penalty:

Advising another to desert; assisting knowingly, or persuading another
to desert.  D. D.; C.—1 yr.

## Entertaining A Deserter

361.  ART. 60.  Any officer who, after having discovered
that a soldier in his command is a deserter from the military or naval service or from the Marine Corps, retains
such deserter in his command without informing superior
authority or the commander of the organization to which
the deserter belongs, shall be punished as a court-martial
may direct.

## Absence Without Leave

362.  ART. 61.  Any person subject to military law who fails
to repair at the fixed time to the properly appointed place of
duty, or goes from the same without proper leave, or absents

himself from his command, guard, quarters, station, or camp without proper leave, shall be punished as a court-martial may direct.

### Penalty:

Absence without leave:
  From command, quarters, station, or camp:
    For not more than 30 days, for each day or fraction of a day of absence. C.—3 days; F. 2 days.
    For more than 30 days. D. D.; C.—6 mo.
  From guard:
    For not more than 1 hour. F.—15 days.
    For more than 1 hour. C.—3 mo.; F. ⅔—3 mo.
Failing to repair at the fixed time to the properly appointed place of assembly for, or place for:
  Athletic exercise; drill; fatigue; field exercise; gallery practice; guard mounting; horse exercise; inspection; instruction; muster; parade; prison guard; review; school; stable duty; target practice; march; reveille or retreat roll call. F.—3 days.
Leaving without permission the properly appointed place of assembly for, or place for:
  Athletic exercise; drill; fatigue; field exercise; gallery practice; guard mounting; horse exercise; inspection; instruction; muster; parade; prison guard; review; school; stable duty; target practice; reveille or retreat roll call. F.—5 days.

## Disrespect Toward the President, Vice-President, Congress, Secretary of War, Governors, Legislatures

**363. ART. 62.** Any officer who uses contemptuous or disrespectful words against the President, Vice President, the Congress of the United States, the Secretary of War, or the governor or legislature of any State, Territory, or other possession of the United States in which he is quartered shall be dismissed from the service or suffer such other punishment as a court-martial may direct. Any other person subject to military law who so offends shall be punished as a court-martial may direct.

### Penalty:

Using contemptuous or disrespectful words against the President, Vice President, etc. D. D.; C.—1 year.

## Disrespect Toward Superior Officers

**364. ART. 63.** Any person subject to military law who behaves himself with disrespect toward his superior officer shall be punished as a court-martial may direct.

### Penalty:

Behaving with disrespect toward his superior officer. C.—6 mo.; F. ⅔—6 mo.

## Assaulting or Willfully Disobeying Superior Officer

**365. ART. 64.** Any person subject to military law who, on any pretense whatsoever, strikes his superior officer or draws or lifts up any weapon or offers any violence against him, being in the execution of his office, or willfully disobeys any lawful command of his superior officer, shall suffer death or such other punishment as a court-martial may direct.

## Insubordinate Conduct Toward Noncommissioned Officer

**366. ART. 65.** Any soldier who strikes or assaults, or who attempts or threatens to strike or asault, or willfully disobeys the lawful order of a noncommissioned officer while in the execution of his office, or uses threatening or insulting language, or behaves in an insubordinate or disrespectful manner toward a noncommissioned officer while in the execution of his office, shall be punished as a court-martial may direct.

### Penalty:

Attempting to strike or attempting otherwise to assault a noncommissioned officer in the execution of his office. C.—6 mo.; F. ⅔—6 mo.

Behaving in an insubordinate or disrespectful manner toward a noncommissioned officer in the execution of his office. C.—2 mo.; F. ⅔—2 mo.

Disobedience, willful, of the lawful order of a noncommissioned officer in the execution of his office. C.—6 mo.; F. ⅔—6 mo.

Striking or otherwise assaulting a noncommissioned officer in the execution of his office. D. D.; C.—1 year.

Threatening to strike or otherwise assault, or using other threatening language toward a noncommissioned officer in the execution of his office. C.—4 mo.; F. ⅔—2 mo.

Using insulting language toward a noncommissioned officer in the execution of his office. C.—2 mo.; F. ⅔—2 mo.

## Mutiny or Sedition

**367. ART. 66.** Any person subject to military law who attempts to create or who begins, excites, causes, or joins in any mutiny or sedition in any company, party, post, camp, detachment, guard, or other command shall suffer death or such other punishment as a court-martial may direct.

## Failure to Suppress Mutiny or Sedition

**368. ART. 67.** Any officer or soldier who, being present at any mutiny or sedition, does not use his utmost endeavor to suppress the same, or knowing or having reason to believe that a mutiny or sedition is to take place, does not without delay give information thereof to his commanding officer shall suffer death or such other punishment as a court-martial may direct.

## Quarrels, Frays, Disorders

**369. Art. 68.** All officers and noncommissioned officers have power to part and quell all quarrels, frays, and disorders among persons subject to military law and to order officers who take part in the same into arrest, and other persons subject to military law who take part in the same into arrest or confinement, as circumstances may require, until their proper superior officer is acquainted therewith. And whosoever, being so ordered, refuses to obey such officer or noncommissioned officer or draws a weapon upon or otherwise threatens or does violence to him shall be punished as a court-martial may direct.

**Penalty:**

Drawing a weapon upon a noncommissioned officer quelling a quarrel, fray, or disorder. D. D.; C.—5 yrs.

Refusing to obey a noncommissioned officer quelling a quarrel, fray, or disorder. D. D.; C.—2 yrs.

Threatening a noncommissioned officer quelling a quarrel, fray, or disorder. C.—6 mo.; F. ⅔—6 mo.

## Arrest or Confinement of Accused Persons

**370. Art. 69.** An officer charged with crime or with a serious offense under these articles shall be placed in arrest by the commanding officer, and in exceptional cases an officer so charged may be placed in confinement by the same authority. A soldier charged with crime or with a serious offense under these articles shall be placed in confinement and when charged with a minor offense he may be placed in arrest. Any other person subject to military law charged with crime or with a serious offense under these articles shall be placed in confinement or in arrest, as circumstances may require; and when charged with a minor offense such person may be placed in arrest. Any person placed in arrest under the provisions of this article shall thereby be restricted to his barracks, quarters, or tent, unless such limits shall be enlarged by proper authority. Any officer who breaks his arrest or who escapes from confinement before he is set at liberty by proper authority shall be dismissed from the service or suffer such other punishment as a court-martial may direct; and any other person subject to military law who escapes from confinement or who breaks his arrest before he is set at liberty by proper authority shall be punished as a court-martial may direct.

**Penalty:**

Breach of arrest. C.—1 mo.; F. ⅔—1 mo.

Escaping from confinement. D. D.; C.—1 yr.

## Investigation of and Action Upon Charges

**371.** Art. No person put in arrest shall be continued in confinement more than eight days, or until such time as a court-martial can be assembled. When any person is put in arrest for the purpose of trial, except at remote military posts or stations, the officer by whose order he is arrested shall see that a copy of the charges on which he is to be tried is served upon him within eight days after his arrest, and that he is brought to trial within 10 days thereafter, unless the necessities of the service prevent such trial; and then he shall be brought to trial within 30 days after the expiration of said 10 days. If a copy of the charges be not served, or the arrested person be not brought to trial, as herein required, the arrest shall cease. But persons released from arrest, under the provisions of this article, may be tried, whenever the exigencies of the service shall permit, within 12 months after such release from arrest: *Provided,* That in time of peace no person shall, against his objection, be brought to trial before a general court-martial within a period of five days subsequent to the service of charges upon him.

## Refusal to Receive and Keep Prisoners

**372.** Art. 71. No provost marshal or commander of a guard shall refuse to receive or keep any prisoner committed to his charge by an officer belonging to the forces of the United States, provided the officer committing shall, at the time, deliver an account in writing, signed by himself, of the crime or offense charged against the prisoner. Any officer or soldier so refusing shall be punished as a court-martial may direct.

## Report of Prisoners Received

**373.** Art. 72. Every commander of a guard to whose charge a prisoner is committed shall, within 24 hours after such confinement, or as soon as he is relieved from his guard, report in writing to the commanding officer the name of such prisoner, the offense charged against him, and the name of the officer committing him; and if he fails to make such report he shall be punished as a court-martial may direct.

## Releasing Prisoner Without Proper Authority

**374.** Art. 73. Any person subject to military law who, without proper authority, releases any prisoner duly committed to his charge, or who, through neglect or design, suffers any prisoner so committed to escape, shall be punished as a court-martial may direct.

**Penalty:**
Releasing, without proper authority, a prisoner committed to his charge.
D. D.; C.—1 yr.
Suffering a prisoner committed to his charge to escape:
Through design. D. D.; C.—1 yr.
Through neglect. C.—6 mo.; F. ⅔—6 mo.

## Delivery of Offenders to Civil Authorities

375. ART. 74. When any person subject to military law, except one who is held by the military authorities to answer, or who is awaiting trial or result of trial, or who is undergoing sentence for a crime or offense punishable under these articles, is accused of a crime or offense committed within the geographical limits of the States of the Union and the District of Columbia, and punishable by the laws of the land, the commanding officer is required, except in time of war, upon application duly made, to use his utmost endeavor to deliver over such accused person to the civil authorities, or to aid the officers of justice in apprehending and securing him, in order that he may be brought to trial. Any commanding officer who upon such application refuses or wilfully neglects, except in time of war, to deliver over such accused person to the civil authorities or to aid the officers of justice in apprehending and securing him shall be dismissed from the service or suffer such other punishment as a court-martial may direct.

When under the provisions of this article delivery is made to the civil authorities of an offender undergoing sentence of a court-martial, such delivery, if followed by conviction, shall be held to interrupt the execution of the sentence of the court-martial, and the offender shall be returned to military custody, after having answered to the civil authorities for his offense, for the completion of the said court-martial sentence.

## Misbehavior Before the Enemy

376. ART. 75. Any officer or soldier who misbehaves himself before the enemy, runs away, or shamefully abandons or delivers up any fort, post, camp, guard, or other command which it is his duty to defend or speaks words inducing others to do the like, or casts away his arms or ammunition, or quits his post, or colors to plunder or pillage, or by any means whatsoever occasions false alarms in camp, garrison, or quarters, shall suffer death or such other punishment as a court-martial may direct.

## Subordinates Compelling Commander to Surrender

377. ART. 76. If any commander of any garrison, fort, post, camp, guard, or other command is compelled by the officers or soldiers under his command to give it up to the

enemy or to abandon it, the officers or soldiers so offending shall suffer death or such other punishment as a court-martial may direct.

## Improper Use of Countersign

**378.** ART. 77. Any person subject to military law who makes known the parole or countersign to any person not entitled to receive it according to the rules and discipline of war, or gives a parole or countersign different from that which he received, shall, if the offense be committed in time of war, suffer death or such other punishment as a court-martial may direct.

## Forcing A Safeguard

**379.** ART. 78. Any person subject to military law who, in time of war, forces a safeguard shall suffer death or such other punishment as a court-martial may direct.

## Captured Property to be Secured for Public Service

**380.** ART. 79. All public property taken from the enemy is the property of the United States and shall be secured for the service of the United States, and any person subject to military law who neglects to secure such property or is guilty of wrongful appropriation thereof shall be punished as a court-martial may direct.

## Dealing in Captured or Abandoned Property

**381.** ART. 80. Any person subject to military law who buys, sells, trades, or in any way deals in or disposes of captured or abandoned property, whereby he shall receive or expect any profit, benefit, or advantage to himself or to any other person directly or indirectly connected with himself, or who fails whenever such property comes into his possession or custody or within his control to give notice thereof to the proper authority and to turn over such property to the proper authority without delay, shall, on conviction thereof, be punished by fine or imprisonment, or by such other punishment as a court-martial, military commission, or other military tribunal may adjudge, or by any or all of said penalties.

## Relieving, Corresponding With, or Aiding the Enemy

**382.** ART. 81. Whosoever relieves the enemy with arms, ammunition, supplies, money, or other thing, or knowingly harbors or protects or holds correspondence with or gives intelligence to the enemy, either directly or indirectly, shall suffer death, or such other punishment as a court-martial or military commis-may direct.

## Spies

**383.** ART. 82. Any person who in time of war shall be found lurking or acting as a spy in or about any of the fortifications, posts, quarters, or encampments of any of the armies of the United States, or elsewhere, shall be tried by a general court-martial or by a military commission, and shall, on conviction thereof, suffer death.

*Spies.—(A person can only be considered a spy when, acting clandestinely or on false pretenses, he obtains or endeavors to obtain information in the zone of operations of a belligerent, with the intention of communicating it to the hostile party.*

*Thus, soldiers not wearing a disguise who have penetrated into the zone of operations of the hostile army, for the purpose of obtaining information, are not considered spies; similarly, the following are not considered spies: Soldiers and civilians, carrying out their mission openly, intrusted with the delivery of dispatches intended either for their own army or for the enemy's army. To this class belong likewise persons sent in balloons for the purpose of carrying dispatches and, generally, of maintaining communications between different parts of an army or a territory.)*—Rules of Land Warfare.

## Military Property—Willful or Negligent Loss, Damage, or Wrongful Disposition of

**384.** ART. 83. Any person subject to military law who willfully or through neglect suffers to be lost, spoiled, damaged, or wrongfully disposed of any military property belonging to the United States shall make good the loss or damage and suffer such punishment as a court-martial may direct.

### Penalty:

Suffering, through neglect, military property to be damaged, lost, spoiled, or wrongfully disposed of:
> Of a value of $20 or less. C.—3 mo.; F. ⅔—3 mo.
> Of a value of $50 or less and more than $20. C.—6 mo.; F. ⅔—6 mo.
> Of a value of more than $50. D. D.; C.—1 year.

Suffering, willfully, military property to be damaged, lost, spoiled, or wrongfully disposed of:
> Of a value of $20 or less. C.—6 mo.; F. ⅔—6 mo.
> Of a value of $50 or less and more than $20. D. D.; C.—6 mo.
> Of a value of more than $50. D. D.; C.—2 years.

## Waste or Unlawful Disposition of Military Property Issued to Soldiers

**385.** ART. 84. Any soldier who sells or wrongfully disposes of or willfully or through neglect injures or loses any horse, arms, ammunition, accouterments, equipments, clothing, or other property issued for use in the military service shall be punished as a court-martial may direct.

### Penalty:

Injuring or losing, through neglect, horse, arms, ammunition, accouterments, equipment, clothing, or other property issued for use in the military service, or items belonging to two or more of said classes:

Of a value of $20 or less. C.—3 mo.; F. ⅔—3 mo.
Of a value of $50 or less and more than $20. C.—6 mo.; F. ⅔—6 mo.
Of a value of more than $50. D. D.; C.—1 year.

Injuring or losing, willfully, horse, arms, ammunition, accouterments, equipment, clothing, or other property issued for use in the military service, or items belonging to two or more of said classes:

Of a value of $20 or less. C.—6 mo.; F. ⅔—6 mo.
Of a value of $50 or less and more than $20. D. D.; C.—6 mo.
Of a value of more than $50. D. D.; C.—2 years.

Selling or otherwise wrongfully disposing of horse, arms, ammunition, accouterments, equipment, clothing, or other property issued for use in the military service, or items belonging to two or more of said classes:

Of a value of $20 or less. D. D.; C.—6 mo.
Of a value of $50 or less and more than $20. D. D.; C.—1 year.
Of a value of more than $50. D. D.; C.—5 years.

## Drunk on Duty

**386.** ART. 85. Any officer who is found drunk on duty shall, if the offense be committed in time of war, be dismissed from the service and suffer such other punishment as a court-martial may direct; and if the offense be committed in time of peace he shall be punished as a court-martial may direct. Any person subject to military law, except an officer, who is found drunk on duty shall be punished as a court-martial may direct.

### Penalty:

Found drunk:
  At formation for or at:
    Athletic exercise; drill; fatigue; field exercise; gallery practice; guard mounting; horse exercise; inspection; instruction; march; muster; parade; review; school; stable duty; target practice; F.—20 days.
  Reveille or retreat roll call. F.—5 days.
  On guard. C.—6 mo.; F. ⅔—6 mo.
  On duty as:
    Barrack orderly; company clerk; cook; dining room orderly; farrier; horseshoer; kitchen police; mechanic; mess sergeant; noncommissioned officer in charge of quarters; saddler; stable sergeant; supply sergeant; wagoner. F.—20 days.

## Misbehavior of Sentinel

**387.** ART. 86. Any sentinel who is found drunk or sleeping upon his post, or who leaves it before he is regularly relieved, shall, if the offense be committed in time of war, suffer death or such other punishment as a court-martial may direct; and if the offense be committed in time of peace he shall suffer any punishment, except death, that a court-martial may direct.

**Penalty:**

Found drunk on post, sentinel. D. D.; C.—6 mo.
Leaving before regularly relieved from or sleeping on post, sentinel. D. D.; C.—1 yr. and 1 mo.

## Personal Interest in Sale of Provisions

**388.** ART. 87. Any officer commanding in any garrison, fort, barracks, camp, or other place where troops of the United States may be serving who, for his private advantage, lays any duty or imposition upon or is interested in the sale of any victuals or other necessaries of life brought into such garrison, fort, barracks, camp, or other place for the use of the troops, shall be dismissed from the service and suffer such other punishment as a court-martial may direct.

## Intimidation of Persons Bringing Provisions

**389.** ART. 88. Any person subject to military law who abuses, intimidates, does violence to, or wrongfully interferes with any person bringing provisions, supplies, or other necessaries to the camp, garrison, or quarters of the forces of the United States shall suffer such punishment as a court-martial may direct.

## Good Order to be Maintained and Wrongs Redressed

**390.** ART. 89. All persons subject to military law are to behave themselves orderly in quarters, garrison, camp, and on the march; and any person subject to military law who commits any waste or spoil, or willfully destroys any property whatsoever (unless by order of his commanding officer), or commits any kind of depredation or riot, shall be punished as a court-martial may direct. Any commanding officer who, upon complaint made to him, refuses or omits to see reparation made to the party injured, in so far as the offender's pay shall go toward such reparation, as provided for in article 105, shall be dismissed from the service or otherwise punished as a court-martial may direct.

## Provoking Speeches or Gestures

**391.** ART. 90. No person subject to military law shall use any reproachful or provoking speeches or gestures to another; and any person subject to military law who offends against the provisions of this article shall be punished as a court-martial may direct.

**Penalty:**

Using a provoking or reproachful speech or gesture to another. C.—3 mo.; F. ⅔—3 mo.

## Dueling

**392. ART. 91.** Any person subject to military law who fights or promotes or is concerned in or connives at fighting a duel, or who having knowledge of a challenge sent or about to be sent fails to report the fact promptly to the proper authority, shall, if an officer, be dismissed from the service or suffer such other punishment as a court-martial may direct; and if any other person subject to military law shall suffer such punishment as a court-martial may direct.

## Murder—Rape

**393. ART. 92.** Any person subject to military law who commits murder or rape shall suffer death or imprisonment for life, as a court-martial may direct; but no person shall be tried by court-martial for murder or rape committed within the geographical limits of the States of the Union and the District of Columbia in time of peace.

## Various Crimes

**394. ART. 93.** Any person subject to military law who commits manslaughter, mayhem, arson, burglary, robbery, larceny, embezzlement, perjury, assault with intent to commit any felony, or assault with intent to do bodily harm, shall be punished as a court-martial may direct.

**Penalty:**

Arson. D. D.; C.—20 years.
Assault:
  With intent to do bodily harm. D. D.; C.—5 years.
  With intent to commit any felony except murder or rape. D. D.; C.—20 years.
  With intent to commit murder or rape. D. D.; C.—20 years.
Burglary. D. D.; C.—10 years.
Embezzlement or larceny:
  Of property of a value of $20 or less. D. D.; C.—6 mo.
  Of property of a value of $50 or less, and more than $20. D. D.; C.—1 year.
  Of property of a value of more than $50. D. D.; C.—5 years.
Manslaughter:
  Involuntary, in the commission of an unlawful act not amounting to a felony, or in the commission of a lawful act which might produce death, in an unlawful manner, or without due caution or circumspection.
  Voluntary, upon a sudden quarrel or heat of passion. D. D.; C.—10 years.
Perjury. D. D.; C.—5 years.
Robbery. D. D.; C.—10 years.

## Frauds Against the Government

**395.** ART. 94. ' Any person subject to military law who makes or causes to be made any claim against the United States or any officer thereof, knowing such claim to be false or fraudulent; or

Who presents or causes to be presented to any person in the civil or military service thereof, for approval or payment, any claim against the United States or any officer thereof, knowing such claim to be false or fraudulent; or

Who enters into any agreement or conspiracy to defraud the United States by obtaining, or aiding others to obtain, the allowance or payment of any false or fraudulent claim; or

Who, for the purpose of obtaining, or aiding others to obtain, the approval, allowance, or payment of any claim against the United States or against any officer thereof, makes or uses, or procures, or advises the making or use of, any writing or other paper, knowing the same to contain any false or fraudulent statements; or

Who, for the purpose of obtaining, or aiding others to obtain, the approval, allowance, or payment of any claim against the United States or any officer thereof, makes, or procures, or advises the making of, any oath to any fact or to any writing or other paper, knowing such oath to be false; or

Who, for the purpose of obtaining, or aiding others to obtain, the approval, allowance, or payment of any claim against the United States or any officer thereof, forges or counterfeits, or procures, or advises the forging or counterfeiting of any signature upon any writing or other paper, or uses, or procures, or advises the use of any such signature, knowing the same to be forged or counterfeited; or

Who, having charge, possession, custody, or control of any money or other property of the United States, furnished or intended for the military service thereof, knowingly delivers, or causes to be delivered, to any person having authority to receive the same, any amount thereof less than that for which he receives a certificate or receipt; or .

Who, being authorized to make or deliver any paper certifying the receipt of any property of the United States furnished or intended for the military service thereof, makes or delivers to any person such writing, without having full knowledge of the truth of the statements therein contained and with intent to defraud the United States; or

Who steals, embezzles, knowingly and willfully misappropriates, applies to his own use or benefit, or wrongfully or knowingly sells or disposes of any ordnance, arms, equipments, ammunition, clothing, subsistence stores, money, or other property of the United States furnished or intended for the military service thereof; or

Who knowingly purchases or receives in pledge for any obligation or indebtedness from any soldier, officer, or other person who is a part of or employed in said forces or service, any ordnance, arms, equipment, ammunition, clothing, subsistence stores, or other property of the United States, such soldier, officer, or other person not having lawful right to sell or pledge the same;

Shall, on conviction thereof, be punished by fine or imprisonment, or by such other punishment as a court-martial may adjudge, or by any or all of said penalties. And if any person, being guilty of any of the offenses aforesaid while in the military service of the United States, receives his discharge or is dismissed from the service, he shall continue to be liable to be arrested and held for trial and sentence by a court-martial in the same manner and to the same extent as if he had not received such discharge nor been dismissed.

**Penalty:**

Forging or counterfeiting a signature, making a false oath, and offenses related to either of these. D. D.; C.—5 yrs.
Other cases:
When the amount involved is $50 or less. D. D.; C.—1 yr.
When the amount involved is more than $50. D. D.; C.—5 yrs.

## Conduct Unbecoming an Officer and Gentleman

**396.** ART. 95. Any officer or cadet who is convicted of conduct unbecoming an officer and a gentleman shall be dismissed from the service.

## General Article

**397.** ART. 96. Though not mentioned in these articles, all disorders and neglects to the prejudice of good order and military discipline, all conduct of a nature to bring discredit upon the military service, and all crimes or offenses not capital, of which persons subject to military law may be guilty, shall be taken cognizance of by a general or special or summary court-martial, according to the nature and degree of the offense, and punished at the discretion of such court.

**Penalty:**

Abandoning guard, by member thereof. C.—6 mo.; F. ⅔—6 mo.
Abusing a public animal. C.—3 mo.; F. ⅔—3 mo.
Allowing a prisoner to receive or obtain intoxicating liquor. C.—3 mo.; F ⅔—3 mo.

Appearing in civilian clothing without authority. F.—10 days.

Appearing in unclean uniform, or not in prescribed uniform, or in uniform worn otherwise than in manner prescribed. C.—1 mo.; F. ⅔—1 mo.

Assault. C.—3 mo.; F. ⅔—3 mo.

Assault and battery. C.—6 mo.; F. ⅔—6 mo.

Attempting to escape from confinement. D. D.; C.—3 mo.

Attempting to strike or attempting otherwise to assault a sentinel in the execution of his duty. C.—6 mo.; F. ⅔—6 mo.

Behaving in an insubordinate or disrespectful manner toward a sentinel in the execution of his duty. C.—1 mo.; F. ⅔—1 mo.

Breach of restriction (other than quarantine) to command, quarters, station, or camp. C.—1 mo.; F. ⅔—1 mo.

Carrying a concealed weapon. C.—3 mo.; F. ⅔—1 mo.

Committing a nuisance. C.—3 mo.; F. ⅔—3 mo.

Concealing, destroying, mutilating, obliterating, or removing willfully and unlawfully a public record, or taking and carrying away a public record with intent to conceal, destroy, mutilate, obliterate, remove, or steal the same. D. D.; C.—3 mo.

Conspiring to escape from confinement. D. D.; C.—6 mo.

Destroying, willfully, public property:
Of a value of $20 or less. D. D.; C.—6 mo.
Of a value of $50 or less, and more than $20. D. D.; C.—1 year.
Of a value of more than $50. D. D.; C.—5 years.

Discharging, through carelessness, a firearm. C.—3 mo.; F. ⅔—3 mo.

Disobedience, willful, of the lawful order of a sentinel in the execution of his duty. D. D.; C.—1 year.

Disorderly in command, quarters, station, or camp. C.—1 mo.; F. ⅔—1 mo.

Disorderly under such circumstances as to bring discredit upon the military service. C.—4 mo.; F. ⅔—4 mo.

Drinking liquor with prisoner. C.—2 mo.; F. ⅔—2 mo.

Drunk and disorderly in command, quarters, station, or camp. C.—3 mo.; F. ⅔—3 mo.

Drunk and disorderly under such circumstances as to bring discredit upon the military service. C.—6 mo.; F. ⅔—6 mo.

Drunk in command, quarters, station or camp. F.—15 days.

Drunk under such circumstances as to bring discredit upon the military service. C.—3 mo.; F. ⅔—3 mo.

Drunk, prisoner found. C.—3 mo.; F. ⅔—3 mo.

Failing to obey a lawful order:
Of a superior officer. D. D.; C.—1 year.
Of a noncommissioned officer. C.—6 mo.; F. ⅔—6 mo.
Of a sentinel. C.—6 mo.; F. ⅔—6 mo.

Failing to pay a just debt under such circumstances as to bring discredit upon the military service. D. D.; C.—6 mo.

False official report or statement knowingly made:
By a noncommissioned officer. C.—3 mo.; F. ⅔—3 mo.
By any other soldier. C.—1 mo.; F. ⅔—1 mo.

False swearing. D. D.; C.—3 yrs.

Forgery. D. D.; C.—5 yrs.

Gambling:
By a noncommissioned officer with a person of lower military rank or grade. F. ⅔—3 mo.
In command, quarters, station or camp in violation of orders. C.—2 mo.; F. ⅔—2 mo.

Indecent exposure of person. C.—3 mo.; F. ⅔—3 mo.

Introducing a habit-forming narcotic drug into command, quarters, station or camp:
    For sale. D. D.; C.—2 yrs.
    All other cases. D. D.; C.—1 yr.

Introducing intoxicating liquor into command, quarters, station or camp:
    For sale. C.—6 mo.; F. ⅔—6 mo.
    All other cases. C.—3 mo.; F. ⅔—3 mo.

Loaning money, either as principal or agent, at an usurious rate of interest to another in the military service. F. ⅔—3 mo.

Loitering or sitting down on duty by sentinel. C.—1 mo.; F. ⅔—1 mo.

Obtaining money or other property under false pretenses:
    When the amount obtained is $20 or less. D. D.; C.—6 mo.
    When the amount obtained is $50 or less and more than $20. D. D.; C.—1 yr.
    When the amount obtained is more than $50. D. D.; C.—5 yrs.

Refusing to submit to medical or dental treatment. D. D.; C.—6 mo.

Refusing to submit to a surgical operation. D. D.; C.—1 yr.

Sodomy and other unnatural crimes. D. D.; C.—5 yrs.

Straggling. C.—3 mo.; F. ⅔—3 mo.

Striking or otherwise assaulting a sentinel in the execution of his duty. D. D.; C.—1 yr.

Subornation of perjury. D. D.; C.—5 yrs.

Threatening to strike or otherwise assault or using other threatening language toward a sentinel in the execution of his duty. C.—4 mo.; F. ⅔—4 mo.

Unclean accouterment, arm, clothing, equipment, or other military property, found with. C.—1 mo.; F. ⅔—1 mo.

Using insulting language toward a sentinel in the execution of his duty. C.—3 mo.; F. ⅔—3 mo.

Uttering a forged instrument. D. D.; C.—5 yrs.

Violation of condition of parole by general prisoner. C.—3 mo.

## Disciplinary Powers of Commanding Officers

**398.** ART. 104. Under such regulations as the President may prescribe, and which he may from time to time revoke, alter, or add to, the commanding officer of any detachment, company, or higher command may, for minor offenses not denied by the accused, impose disciplinary punishments upon persons of his command without the intervention of a court-martial, unless the accused demands trial by court-martial.

The disciplinary punishments authorized by this article may include admonition, reprimand, withholding of privileges, extra fatigue, and restriction to certain specified limits, but shall not include forfeiture of pay or confinement under guard. A person punished under authority of this article who deems his punishment unjust or disproportionate to the offense may, through the proper channel, appeal to the next superior authority, but may in the meantime be required to undergo the punishment adjudged. The commanding officer who imposes the punishment, his successor in command, and superior authority shall have power to mitigate or remit any unexecuted portion of the punishment. The imposition and enforcement of disciplinary punishment under authority of this article for any act or omission shall not be a bar to trial by court-martial for a crime or offense growing out of the same act or omission; but the fact that a disciplinary punishment has been enforced may be shown by the accused upon trial, and when so shown shall be considered in determining the measure of punishment to be adjudged in the event of a finding of guilty.

## Redress of Injuries to Person or Property

**399.** ART. 105. Whenever complaint is made to any commanding officer that damage has been done to the property of any person or that his property has been wrongfully taken by persons subject to military law, such complaint shall be investigated by a board consisting of any number of others from one to three, which board shall be convened by the commanding officer and shall have, for the purpose of such investigation, power to summon witnesses and examine them upon oath or affirmation, to receive depositions or other documentary evidence, and to assess the damages sustained against the responsible parties. The assessment of damages made by such board shall be subject to the approval of the commanding officer, and in the amount approved by him shall be stopped against the pay of the offenders. And the order of such commanding officer directing stoppages herein authorized shall be conclusive on any disbursing officer for the payment by him to the injured parties of the stoppages so ordered.

Where the offender can not be ascertained but the organization or detachment to which they belong is known, stoppages to the amount of damages inflicted may be made and assessed in such proportion as may be deemed just upon the individual members thereof who are shown to have been present with such organization or detachment at the time the damages complained of were inflicted, as determined by the approved findings of the board.

## Arrest of Deserters by Civil Officials

**400.** ART. 106. It shall be lawful for any civil officer having authority under the laws of the United States, or of any State, Territory, District, or possession of the United States, to arrest offenders, summarily to arrest a deserter from the military service of the United States and deliver him into the custody of the military authorities of the United States.

## Soldiers to Make Good Time Lost

**401.** ART. 107. Every soldier who in an existing or subsequent enlistment deserts the service of the United States or without proper authority absents himself from his organization, station or duty for more than one day, or who is confined for more than one day under sentence, or while awaiting trial and disposition of his case, if the trial results in conviction, or through the intemperate use of drugs or alcoholic liquor, or through disease or injury the result of his own misconduct, renders himself unable for more than one day to perform duty, shall be liable to serve, after his return to a full-duty status, for such period as shall, with the time he may have served prior to such desertion, unauthorized absence, confinement, or inability to perform duty, amount to the full term of that part of his enlistment period which he is required to serve with his organization before being furloughed to the Army Reserve.

## Soldiers—Separation from the Service

**402.** ART. 108. No enlisted man, lawfully inducted into the military service of the United States, shall be discharged from said service without a certificate of discharge, signed by a field officer of the regiment or other organization to which the enlisted man belongs or by the commanding officer when no such field officer is present; and no enlisted man shall be discharged from said service before his term of service has expired, except by order of the President, the Secretary of War, the commanding officer of a department, or by sentence of a general court-martial.

## Oath of Enlistment

**403.** ART. 109. At the time of his enlistment every soldier shall take the following oath or affirmation: "I, ———, do solemnly swear (or affirm) that I will bear true faith and allegiance to the United States of America; that I will serve them honestly and faithfully against all their enemies whomsoever; and that I will obey the orders of the President of the United States and the orders of the officers appointed over me, according to the Rules and Articles of War." This oath or affirmation may be taken before any officer.

# CHAPTER XII

## PERSONAL HYGIENE AND CARE OF THE FEET

### Personal Hygiene

**404.** History shows that in almost every war many more men die of disease than from wounds received in battle. Much of this disease is preventable and is due either to the ignorance or carelessness of the person who has the disease or of other persons about him. It is a terrible truth that one man who violates any of the great rules of health may be the means of killing many more of his comrades than are killed by the bullets of the enemy.

**It is therefore most important that every soldier should learn how to take care of his health when in the field and that he should also insist that his comrades do not violate any of the rules prescribed for this purpose.**

A great many diseases are due to germs, which are either little animals or little plants so very small that they can only be seen by aid of the microscope. All diseases caused by germs are "catching." All other diseases are not "catching."

There are only five ways of catching disease:

(*a*) Getting certain germs on the body by touching someone or something which has them on it. Thus, one may catch venereal diseases, smallpox, measles, scarlet fever, chicken pox, mumps, boils, body lice, ringworm, barber's itch, dhobie itch, and some other diseases. Wounds are infected in this manner.

(*b*) Breathing in certain germs which float in the air. In this way one may catch pneumonia, consumption, influenza, diphtheria, whooping cough, tonsilitis, spinal meningitis, measles, and certain other diseases.

(*c*) Taking certain germs in through the mouth in eating or drinking. Dysentery, cholera, typhoid fever, diarrhea, and intestinal worms may be caught in this manner.

(*d*) Having certain germs injected into the body by the bites of insects, such as mosquitoes, fleas, and bedbugs. Malaria, yellow fever, dengue fever, and bubonic plague may be caught in this way.

(*e*) Inheriting the germ from one's parents.

Persons may have these germs sometimes without apparently being sick with any disease. Such persons and persons who are sick with the diseases are a great source of danger to others about them. Germs which multiply in such persons are found in their urine and excretions from the bowels; in discharges from ulcers and abscesses; in the spit or particles coughed or sneezed into the air; in the perspiration or scales from the skin; and in the blood sucked up by biting insects.

Those who have taken care of their health and who have not become weakened by bad habits, exposure, and fatigue are not only less liable to catch disease, but are more apt to recover when taken sick.

Knowing all these things, the soldier can understand the reasons for the following rules and how important it is that they should be carried out by each and every person:

Stay away from persons having "catching" diseases.

If you have any disease, don't try to cure it yourself, but go to the surgeon. Insist that other soldiers do likewise.

Typhoid fever is one of the most dangerous and common camp diseases. Modern medicine has, however, discovered an effective preventative for this disease in the typhoid prophylactic, which renders the person immune from typhoid fever. The treatment consists in injecting into the arm a preventative serum. The injection is given three times at 10-day intervals.

Association with lewd women is dangerous. It may result in disabling you for life. It is the cause of a disease (syphilis) which may be transmitted by a parent to his children. Soldiers with venereal diseases should not use basins or toilet articles used by others, as the germs of these diseases if gotton into the eye very often cause blindness. Likewise, if they use the same drinking cup used by others they may give others the disease. They should promptly report their troubles to the surgeon, that they may receive the best medical advice and attention.

Should a soldier expose himself to infection by having intercourse with an unknown woman, he should report as soon as possible afterwards to the regimental infirmary for prophylactic treatment, which, if taken within a few hours after intercourse, will prevent to a large degree the liability of contracting any disease.

Cooked germs are dead and therefore harmless. Water, even when clear, may be alive with deadly germs. Therefore, when the conditions are such that the commanding officer orders all drinking water to be boiled, be careful to live up to this order.

Use the latrines and don't go elsewhere to relieve yourself. In open latrines cover your deposit with dirt, as it breeds flies and may also be full of germs.

Flies carry germs from one place to another. Therefore see that your food and mess kit are protected from them.

All slops and scraps of food scattered about camp soon produce bad odors and draw flies. Therefore do your part toward keeping the camp free from disease by carefully depositing such refuse in the pits or cans used for this purpose.

Urinate only in the latrines, or in the cans set out for this purpose, never on the ground around camp, because it not only causes bad smells but urine sometimes contains the germs of "catching" diseases.

Soapy water thrown on the ground soon produces bad odors. Therefore in camps of several days' duration this water should be thrown in covered pits or in cans used for this purpose.

As certain mosquitoes can transmit malaria and yellow fever, use your mosquito bar for this reason as well as for personal comfort.

Keep your mouth clean by brushing your teeth once or twice a day. It helps to prevent the teeth from decaying. Decayed teeth cause toothache. They also lead one to swallow food without properly chewing it, and this leads to stomach troubles of various kinds. Food left around and between the teeth is bad for the teeth and forms good breeding places for germs.

Keep the skin clean. Through the pores of the skin the body gets rid of much waste and poisonous matter. Therefore remove this and keep the pores open by bathing once every day, if possible. If water is scarce rub the body over with a wet towel. If no water is at hand, take a dry rub. Wash carefully the armpits, between the legs, and under the foreskin, as this will prevent chafing.

The skin protects the sentitive parts underneath from injury and helps to keep out germs. Therefore when blisters are formed don't tear off the skin. Insert a needle under the skin a little distance back from the blister and push it through to the opposite side. Press out the liquid through the holes thus formed. Heat the needle red hot first, with a match or candle, to kill the germs.

When the skin is broken (in cuts and wounds) keep the opening covered with a bandage to keep out germs and dirt; otherwise the sore may fester. Pus is always caused by germs.

Keep your hair short. Long hair and a long beard in the field generally means a dirty head and a dirty face and favors skin diseases, lice and dandruff.

Don't let any part of the body become chilled, as this very often is the direct cause of diarrhea, dysentery, pneumonia, rheumatism, and other diseases.

Wet clothes may be worn while marching or exercising without bad results, but there is great danger if one rests in wet clothing, as the body may become chilled.

Don't sit or lie or sleep directly on damp ground, as this is sure to chill the body.

When hot or perspiring or when wearing damp clothes, don't remain where a breeze can strike you. You are sure to become chilled.

Every day, if possible, hang your blanket and clothing out to air in the sun; shake or beat them with a small stick. Germs and vermin don't like this treatment, but damp, musty clothing suits them very well. Wash your shirts, underwear, and socks frequently. The danger of blood poisoning from a wound is greatly increased if the bullet passes through dirty clothes.

Ditch your tent as soon as you can, particularly a shelter tent, even if you camp for one night only. Otherwise a little rain may ruin a whole night's rest.

Always prepare your bed before dark. Level off the ground and scrape out a little hollow for your hips. Get some straw or dry grass if possible. Green grass or branches from trees are better than nothing. Sleep on your poncho. This keeps the dampness from coming up from the ground and chilling the body. Every minute spent in making a good bed means about an hour's good rest later on.

Avoid the food and drink found for sale in the cheap stands about camp. The quality is generally bad, and it is often prepared in filthy places by very dirty persons.

The use of intoxicating liquor is particularly dangerous in the field. Its excessive use, even at long intervals, breaks down one's system. Drinking men are more apt to get sick and less liable to get well than are their more sober comrades. If alcohol is taken at all, it is best after the work of the day is over. It should never be taken when the body is exposed to severe cold, as it diminishes the resistance of the body. Hot tea or coffee is much preferable under these circumstances.

## Care of the Feet

**405.** A soldier can not march with sore feet, and marching is the main part of an infantryman's daily duty in the field.

All soldiers should be familiar with the proper methods of caring for the feet. Sore feet are generally due to carelessness, neglect, or ignorance on the part of the soldier.

The most important factor in the care of the feet and the marching ability of the soldier is the shoe. Civilian shoes, particularly light, patent leather, or low shoes, are sure to cause injury and in time will ruin a man's foot. Only the marching shoe issued by the Quartermaster Corps should be worn, and they must be properly fitted to the individual. It will not suffice to order a marching shoe of the same size as one's ordinary civilian shoes, for it must be remembered that a soldier may have to march many miles daily over rough roads and carrying a heavy pack. The pack itself causes the foot to spread out to a larger size, and the rough roads give so much exercise to the muscles of the feet that they swell greatly through the increased blood supply. (For directions as to measuring the foot for the marching shoe see General Order No. 26, War Department, 1912, a copy of which should be on hand in each company.)

Do not start out on a march wearing new shoes. This is a frequent cause of sore feet. New shoes should be properly broken in before beginning a march by wearing them for several hours daily for a week before the march, and they should be adapted to the contours of the feet by stretching them with shoe stretchers with adjustable knobs to take the pressure off painful corns and bunions. Such stretchers are issued by the Quartermaster Corps, and there should be one or more pair in every company of infantry. Should this be impracticable, then the following is suggested:

The soldier stands in his new shoes in about 2½ inches of water for about five minutes until the leather is thoroughly pliable and moist; he should then walk for about an hour on a level surface, letting the shoes dry on his feet, to the irregularities of which the leather is thus molded in the same way as it was previously molded over the shoe last. On taking the shoes off a very little neat's foot oil should be rubbed into the leather to prevent its hardening and cracking.

If it is desired to waterproof shoes at any time, a considerable amount of neat's-foot oil should be rubbed into the leather. Waterproof leather causes the feet of some men to perspire unduly and keeps them constantly soft.

Light woolen or heavy woolen socks will habitually be worn for marching. Cotton socks will not be worn unless specifically ordered by the surgeon. The socks will be large enough to permit free movement of the toes, but not so loose as to permit of wrinkling. Darned socks, or socks with holes in them, will not be worn in marching.

Until the feet have hardened they should be dusted with foot powder, which can be obtained at the regimental infirmary, before each day's march. Clean socks should be worn daily.

As soon as possible after reaching camp after a day of marching the feet should be washed with soap and water, and the soldier should put on a dry pair of socks and his extra pair of shoes from his surplus kit. If the skin is tender, or the feet perspire, wash with warm salt water or alum water, but do not soak the feet a long time, as this, although very comforting at the time, tends to keep them soft. Should blisters appear on the feet, prick and evacuate them by pricking at the lower edge with a pin which has been passed through the flame of a match and cover them with zinc oxide plaster applied hot. This plaster can be obtained on request at the regimental infirmary. If serious abrasions appear on the feet, or corns, bunions, and ingrowing nails cause trouble, have your name placed on sick report and apply to the surgeon for treatment. Cut the toe nails square (fairly close in the middle, but leaving the sides somewhat longer), as this prevents ingrowing nails.

# CHAPTER XIII

## GUARD DUTY

406. This chapter is based on the Manual of Interior Guard Duty, issued by the War Department. A number of copies of this book are supplied to Companies and the guard, at every place where troops are stationed is furnished with a few copies.

The soldier rarely ever sees the book except when he is performing a tour of guard duty and then only for a few moments at a time. He is afforded no real opportunity for studying the subject. He learns it by experience and by going through the process of being "skinned" for his failure to observe this or that rule. Take this chapter and read it over. Give it a little thought and study. Make sure that you understand what is intended and you will have less trouble with your tours of guard duty.

The numbers following the several paragraphs refer to corresponding paragraphs in the Manual of Guard Duty.

### Sergeant of the Guard

The senior noncommissioned officer of the guard always acts as sergeant of the guard, and if there be no officer of the guard, will perform the duties prescribed for the commander of the guard. (80)

The sergeant of the guard has general supervision over the other noncommissioned officers and the musicians and privates of the guard, and must be thoroughly familiar with all of their orders and duties. (81)

He is directly responsible for the property under charge of the guard, and will see that it is properly cared for. He will make lists of articles taken out by working parties and see that all such articles are duly returned. If they are not, he will immediately report the fact to the commander of the guard. (82)

Immediately after guard mounting he will prepare duplicate lists of the names of all noncommissioned officers, musicians, and privates of the guard, showing the relief and post or duties of each. One list will be handed as soon as possible to the commander of the guard; the other will be retained by the sergeant. (83)

He will see that all reliefs are turned out at the proper time, and that the corporals thoroughly understand, and are prompt and efficient in, the discharge of their duties. (84)

During the temporary absence from the guardhouse of the sergeant of the guard, the next in rank of the noncommissioned officers will perform his duties. (85)

Should the corporal whose relief is on post be called away from the guardhouse, the sergeant of the guard will designate a noncommissioned officer to take the corporal's place until his return. (86)

The sergeant of the guard is responsible at all times for the proper police of the guardhouse or guard tent, including the ground about them and the prison cells. (87)

At first sergeant's call he will proceed to the adjutant's office and obtain the guard report book. (88)

When the national or regimental colors are taken from the stacks of the color line, the color bearer and guard, or the sergeant of the guard, unarmed, and two armed privates as a guard, will escort the colors to the colonel's quarters, as prescribed for the color guard in the drill regulations of the arm of the service to which the guard belongs. (89)

He will report to the commander of the guard any suspicious or unusual occurrence that comes under his notice, will warn him of the approach of any armed body, and will send to him all persons arrested by the guard. (90)

When the guard is turned out its formation will be as follows: The senior noncommissioned officer, if commander of the guard, is on the right of the right guide; if not commander of the guard, he is in the line of file closers, in rear of the right four of the guard; the next in rank is right guide; the next left guide; the others in the line of file closers, usually each in rear of his relief; the field music, with its left three paces to the right of the right guide. The reliefs form in the same order as when the guard was first divided, except that if the guard consists of dismounted cavalry and infantry, the cavalry forms on the left. (91)

The sergeant forms the guard, calls the roll, and, if not in command of the guard, reports to the commander of the guard as prescribed in drill regulations for a first sergeant forming a troop or company; the guard is not divided into platoons or sections, and, except when the whole guard is formed prior to marching off, fours are not counted. (92)

The sergeant reports as follows: *"Sir, all present or accounted for,"* or *"Sir, (so-and-so) is absent,"* or if the roll call has been omitted, *"Sir, the guard is formed."* Only men absent without proper authority are reported absent. He then takes his place, without command. (93)

, At night the roll may be called by reliefs and numbers instead of names; thus, the first relief being on post: *Second relief; No.* 1; *No.* 2, *etc.; Third relief, Corporal; No.* 1, *etc.* (94)

Calling the roll will be dispensed with in forming the guard when it is turned out as a compliment, on the approach of an armed body, or in any sudden emergency; but in such cases the roll may be called before dismissing the guard. If the guard be turned out for an officer entitled to inspect it, the roll will, unless he directs otherwise, always be called before a report is made. (95)

The sergeant of the guard has direct charge of the prisoners, except during such time as they may be under the charge of the prisoner guard or overseers, and is responsible to the commander of the guard for their security. (96)

He will carry the keys of the guardroom and cells, and will not suffer them to leave his personal possession while he is at the guardhouse, except as hereinafter provided. (Par. 99.) Should he leave the guardhouse for any purpose he will turn the keys over to the noncommissioned officer who takes his place. (Par. 85.) (97)

He will count the knives, forks, etc., given to the prisoners with their food, and see that none of these articles remain in their possession. He will see that no forbidden articles of any kind are conveyed to the prisoners. (98)

Prisoners when paraded with the guard are placed in line, in its center. The sergeant, immediately before forming the guard, will turn over his keys to the noncommissioned officer at the guardhouse. Having formed the guard, he will divide it into two nearly equal parts. Indicating the point of division with his hand, he commands: 1. *Right (or left),* 2. *FACE,* 3. *Forward,* 4, *MARCH,* 5. *Guard,* 6. *HALT,* 7. *Left (or right),* 8, *FACE.*

If the first command be *right face,* the right half of the guard only will execute the movements; if *left face,* the left half only will execute them. The command *halt* is given when sufficient interval is obtained to admit the prisoners. The doors of the guardroom and cells are then opened by the non-commissioned officer having the keys. The prisoners will file out under the supervision of the sergeant, the noncommissioned officer, and sentinel on duty at the guardhouse, and such other sentinels as may be necessary; they will form in line in the interval between the two parts of the guard. (99)

To return the prisoners to the guardroom and cells, the sergeant commands: 1. *Prisoners,* 2. *Right (or left),* 3. *FACE,* 4. *Column right (or left),* 5. *MARCH.* (100)

The prisoners, under the same supervision as before, return to their proper rooms or cells.

To close the guard, the sergeant commands: 1. *Left (or right),* 2. *FACE,* 3. *Forward,* 4. *MARCH,* 5. *Guard,* 6. *HALT,* 7. *Right (or left),* 8. *FACE.* (101)

The left or right half only of the guard, as indicated, executes the movement.

If there be but few prisoners, the sergeant may indicate the point of division as above, and form the necessary interval by the commands: 1. *Right (or left) step,* 2. *MARCH,* 3. *Guard,* 4. *HALT,* and close the intervals by the commands: 1. *Left (or right) step,* 2. *MARCH,* 3. *Guard,* 4. *HALT.* (102)

If sentinels are numerous, reliefs may, at the discretion of the commanding officer, be posted in detachments, and sergeants, as well as corporals, required to relieve and post them. (103)

## Corporal of the Guard

A corporal of the guard receives and obeys orders from none but noncommissioned officers of the guard senior to himself, the officers of the guard, the officer of the day, and the commanding officer. (104)

It is the duty of the corporal of the guard to post and relieve sentinels and to instruct the members of his relief in their orders and duties. (105)

Immediately after the division of the guard into reliefs the corporals will assign the members of their respective reliefs to posts by number, and a soldier so assigned to his post will not be changed to another during the same tour of guard duty, unless by direction of the commander of the guard or higher authority. Usually, experienced soldiers are placed over the arms of the guard, and at remote and responsible posts. (106)

Each corporal will then make a list of the members of his relief including himself. This list will contain the number of the relief, the name, the company, and the regiment of every member thereof, and the post to which each is assigned. The list will be made in duplicate, one copy to be given to the sergeant of the guard as soon as completed, the other to be retained by the corporal. (107)

When directed by the commander of the guard, the corporal of the first relief forms his relief, and then commands: *CALL OFF*.

Commencing on the right, the men call off alternately *rear* and *front rank,* "one," "two," "three," "four," and so on; if in single rank, they call of from right to left. The corporal then commands: 1. *Right,* 2. *Face,* 3. *Forward,* 4. *MARCH*.

The corporal marches on the left, and near the rear file, in order to observe the march. The corporal of the old guard marches on the right of the leading file, and takes command when the last one of the old sentinels is relieved, changing places with the corporal of the new guard. (108)

When the relief arrives at six paces from a sentinel (see par. 168), the corporal halts it and commands, according to the number of the post: *No. (——.)*

Both sentinels execute port arms or saber; the new sentinel approaches the old, halting about one pace from him. (See par. 172.)   (109)

The corporals advance and place themselves, facing each other. a little in advance of the new sentinel, the old corporal on his right, the new corporal on his left, both at a right shoulder, and observe that the old sentinel transmits correctly his instructions.

The following diagram will illustrate the positions taken:

$$\overline{A}$$

**R**

| | | | |         C |      —**D**
| | | |

$$\overline{B}$$

R is the relief; A, the new corporal; B, the old; C, the new sentinel; D, the old.   (110)

The instructions relative to the post having been communicated, the new corporal commands. *Post:* both sentinels then resume the right shoulder, face toward the new corporal and step back so as to allow the relief to pass in front of them. The new corporal then commands: "1. *Forward,* 2. *March;*" the old sentinel takes his place in rear of the relief as it passes him, his piece in the same position as those of the relief. The new sentinel stands fast at a right shoulder until the relief has passed six paces beyond him, when he walks his post. The corporals take their places as the relief passes them.   (111)

Mounted sentinels are posted and relieved in accordance with the same principles.   (112)

On the return of the old relief, the corporal of the new guard falls out when the relief halts; the corporal of the old guard forms his relief on the left of the old guard, salutes and reports to the commander of his guard: *"Sir, the relief is present;"* or *"Sir, (so and so) is absent,"* and takes his place in the guard. (113)

To post a relief other than that which is posted when the old guard is relieved, its corporal commands:

1. *(Such) relief,* 2. *FALL IN;* and if arms are stacked, they are taken at the proper commands.

The relief is formed facing to the front, with arms at an order, the men place themselves according to the numbers of their respective posts, viz. *two, four, six,* and so on, in the *front rank,* and *one, three, five,* and so on, in the *rear rank.* The corporal standing about two paces in front of the center of his relief, then commands: *CALL OFF.*

The men call off as prescribed. The corporal then commands: 1. *Inspection,* 2. *ARMS,* 3. *Order,* 4. *ARMS;* faces the commander of the guard, executes the rifle salute, reports: *"Sir, the relief is present;"* or *"Sir, (so and so) is absent;"* he then takes his place on the right at order arms. (114)

When the commander of the guard directs the corporal, *Post your relief,* the corporal salutes and posts his relief as prescribed (Pars. 108 to 111); the corporal of the relief on post does not go with the new relief, except when necessary to show the way. (115)

To dismiss the old relief, it is halted and faced to the front at the guardhouse by the corporal of the new relief, who then falls out; the corporal of the old relief then steps in front of the relief and dismisses it by the proper commands. (116)

Should the pieces have been loaded before the relief was posted, the corporal will, before dismissing the relief, see that no cartridges are left in the chambers or magazines. The same rule applies to sentinels over prisoners. (117)

Each corporal will thoroughly acquaint himself with all the special orders of every sentinel on his relief, and see that each understands and correctly transmits such orders in detail to his successor. (118)

There should be at least one noncommissioned officer constantly on the alert at the guardhouse, usually the corporal whose relief is on post. This noncommissioned officer takes post near the entrance of the guardhouse, and does not fall in with the guard when it is formed. He will have his rifle constantly with him. (119)

Whenever it becomes necessary for the corporal to leave his post near the entrance of the guardhouse, he will notify the sergeant of the guard, who will at once take his place, or designate another noncommissioned officer to do so. (120)

He will see that no person enters the guardhouse or guard tent, or crosses the posts of the sentinels there posted without proper authority. (121)

Should any sentinel call for the corporal of the guard, the corporal will, in every case, at once and quickly proceed to such sentinel. He will notify the sergeant of the guard before leaving the guardhouse. (122)

He will at once report to the commander of the guard any violation of regulations or any unusual occurrence which is reported to him by a sentinel, or which comes to his notice in any other way. (123)

Should a sentinel call "The Guard," the corporal will promptly notify the commander of the guard. (124)

Should a sentinel call "Relief," the corporal will at once proceed to the post of such sentinel, taking with him the man next for duty on that post. If the sentinel is relieved for a short time only, the corporal will again post him as soon as the necessity for his relief ceases. (125)

When the countersign is used, the corporal at the posting of the relief during whose tour challenging is to begin, gives the countersign to the members of the relief, excepting those posted at the guardhouse. (126)

He will wake the corporal whose relief is next on post in time for the latter to verify the prisoners, form his relief, and post it at the proper hour. (127)

Should the guard be turned out, each corporal will call his own relief, and cause its members to fall in promptly. (128)

Tents or bunks in the same vicinity will be designated for the reliefs so that all the members of each relief may, if necessary, be found and turned out by the corporal in the least time and with the least confusion. (129)

When challenged by a sentinel while posting his relief, the corporal commands: 1. *Relief,* 2. *HALT;* to the sentinel's challenge he answers "Relief," and at the order of the sentinel he advances alone to give the countersign, or to be recognized. When the sentinel says, "Advance relief," the corporal commands: 1. *Forward,* 2. *MARCH.* (130)

If to be relieved, the sentinel is then relieved as prescribed.

Between retreat and reveille, the corporal of the guard will challenge all suspicious looking persons or parties he may observe, first halting his patrol or relief, if either be with him. He will advance them in the same manner that sentinels on post advance like parties (pars. 191 to 197), but if the route of a patrol is on a continuous chain of sentinels, he should not challenge persons coming near him unless he has reason to believe that they have eluded the vigilance of sentinels. (131)

Between retreat and reveille, whenever so ordered by an officer entitled to inspect the guard, the corporal will call: *"Turn out the guard,"* announcing the title of the officer, and then, if not otherwise ordered, he will salute and return to his post. (132)

As a general rule he will advance parties approaching the guard at night in the same manner that sentinels on post advance like parties. Thus, the sentinel at the guardhouse challenges and repeats the answer to the corporal, as prescribed hereafter (par. 200); the corporal, advancing at port arms, says: *"Advance (so and so) with the countersign,"* or *"to be recognized,"* if there be no countersign used; the countersign being correctly given, or the party being duly recognized, the corporal says: *"Advance (so and so),"* repeating the answer to the challenge of the sentinel. (133)

When officers of different rank approach the guardhouse from different directions at the same time, the senior will be advanced first, and will not be made to wait for his junior. (134)

Out of ranks and under arms, the corporal salutes with the rifle salute. He will salute all officers, whether by day or night. (135)

The corporal will examine parties halted and detained by sentinels, and, if he has reason to believe the parties have no authority to cross sentinel's posts, will conduct them to the commander of the guard. (136)

The corporal of the guard will arrest all suspicious looking characters prowling about the post or camp, all persons of a disorderly character disturbing the peace, and all persons taken in the act of committing crime against the Government on a military reservation or post. All persons arrested by corporals of the guard or by sentinels will at once be conducted to the commander of the guard by the corporal. (137)

### Musicians of the Guard

The musicians of the guard will sound calls as prescribed by the commanding officer. (138)

Should the guard be turned out for national or regimental colors or standards, uncased, the field music of the guard will, when the guard present arms, sound, *"To the color"* or *"To the standard;"* or, if for any person entitled thereto, the march, flourishes, or ruffles. (139)

1. *The President of the United States will be received with regimental standards or colors, officers and troops saluting, the drums giving four ruffles and the bugles sounding four flourishes. The ruffles and flourishes will be followed by the National Anthem, or, in the absence of a band, the field music or bugles will sound "To the Color."*

2. *An ex-President, and the Vice President of the United States will be received with the same honors as prescribed for the President, except that the flourishes will be followed by a march in lieu of the National Anthem.*

3. *The President of a foreign Republic, a foreign sovereign, or a member of a Royal family will be received with the same honors as prescribed in par. 1, except that the National Anthem of his country will be played.*

4. *Officers of the following grades of rank will be received with regimental standards or colors, officers and troops saluting, and field music playing as follows: General, four ruffles and flourishes; Lieutenant General, three ruffles and flourishes; Major General, two ruffles and flourishes; Brigadier General, one ruffle and flourish.*

*In tendering honors to a general officer or official of like rank, the General's March will be played immediately after the flourishes.*

*To the members of the Cabinet, the Chief Justice, the President pro-tempore of the Senate, the Speaker of the House of Representatives, American or foreign ambassadors, and Governors within their respective States and Territories, the same honors are paid as to the General, except that a foreign Ambassador will be received with the national anthem of his country, and that the number of guns fired as personal salutes will be as prescribed in Paragraph 400 of the Army Regulations; to the Assistant Secretary of War, and to American or Foreign envoys or ministers the same honors as to the Lieutenant General; to officers of the Navy the honors due to their relative rank; to officers of the Marines and Volunteers and Militia, when in the service of the United States, the honors due to like grades in the regular service; to officers of a foreign service, the honors due to their rank.*

*In rendering personal honors, when the command presents arms, officers and men in uniform who are not in formation*

*and are in view and within saluting distance shall salute and
shall remain in the position of salute until the end of the
ruffles and flourishes or, if none, until "Order Arms."*

## Orderlies and Color Sentinels

When so directed by the commanding officer, the officer who
inspects the guard at guard mounting will select from the
members of the new guard an orderly for the commanding
officer and such number of other orderlies and color sentinels
as may be required. (140)

For these positions the soldiers will be chosen who are most
correct in the performance of duty and in military bearing,
neatest in person and clothing, and whose arms and accouterments are in the best condition. Clothing, arms, and equipments must conform to regulations. If there is any doubt as
to the relative qualifications of two or more soldiers, the inspecting officer will cause them to fall out at the guardhouse
and to form in line in single rank. He will then, by testing
them in drill regulations, select the most proficient. The commander of the guard will be notified of the selection. (141)

When directed by the commander of the guard to fall out
and report an orderly will give his name, company, and regiment to the sergeant of the guard, and, leaving his rifle in the
arm rack in his company quarters, will proceed at once to
the officer to whom he is assigned, reporting: *"Sir, Private
———, Company ———, reports as orderly."* (142)

If the orderly selected be a cavalryman, he will leave his
rifle in the arm rack of his troop quarters, and report with
his belt on, but without side arms unless specially otherwise
ordered. (143)

Orderlies, while on duty as such, are subject only to the
orders of the commanding officer and of the officers to whom
they are ordered to report. (144)

When an orderly is ordered to carry a message, he will be
careful to deliver it exactly as it was given to him. (145)

His tour of duty ends when he is relieved by the orderly
selected from the guard relieving his own. (146)

Orderlies are members of the guard, and their name, company, and regiment are entered on the guard report and lists
of the guard. (147)

If a color line is established, sufficient sentinels are placed
on the color line to guard the colors and stacks. (148)

Color sentinels are posted only so long as the stacks are
formed. The commander of the guard will divide the time
equally among them. (149)

When stacks are broken, the color sentinels may be permitted to return to their respective companies. They are required to report in person to the commander of the guard at reveille and retreat. They will fall in with the guard, under arms, at guard mounting. (150)

Color sentinels are not placed on the regular reliefs, nor are their posts numbered. In calling for the corporal of the guard, they call: *"Corporal of the guard. Color line."* (151)

Officers or enlisted men passing the uncased colors will render the prescribed salute. If the colors are on the stacks, the salute will be made on crossing the color line or on passing the colors. (152)

A sentinel placed over the colors will not permit them to be moved except in the presence of an armed escort. Unless otherwise ordered by the commanding officer, he will allow no one to touch them but the color bearer.

He will not permit any soldier to take arms from the stacks or to touch them except by order of an officer or noncommissioned officer of the guard.

If any person passing the colors or crossing the color line fails to salute the colors, the sentinel will caution him to do so, and if the caution be not heeded he will call the corporal of the guard and report the facts. (153)

## Privates of the Guard

Privates are assigned to reliefs by the commander of the guard, and to posts usually by the corporal of their relief. They will not change from one relief or post to another during the same tour of guard duty unless by proper authority. (154)

## Orders for Sentinels

Orders for sentinels are of two classes: General orders and special orders. General orders apply to all sentinels. Special orders relate to particular posts and duties. (155)

Sentinels will be required to memorize the following:

My general orders are:

## 1. To take charge of this post and all Government property in view.

## 2. To walk my post in a military manner keeping always on the alert and observing

everything that takes place within sight or hearing.

3. To report all violations of orders I am instructed to enforce.

4. To repeat all calls from posts more distant from the guardhouse than my own.

5. To quit my post only when properly relieved.

6. To receive, obey, and pass on to the sentinel who relieves me all orders from the commanding officer, officer of the day, and officers and noncommissioned officers of the guard only.

7. To talk to no one except in line of duty.

8. In case of fire or disorder to give the alarm.

9. To allow no one to commit a nuisance on or near my post.

10. In any case not covered by instructions to call the corporal of the guard.

11. To salute all officers, and all colors and standards not cased.

12. To be especially watchful at night, and during the time for challenging, to challenge all persons on or near my post and to allow no one to pass without proper authority. (156)

## REGULATIONS RELATING TO THE GENERAL ORDERS FOR SENTINELS

**No. 1: To take charge of this post and all Government property in view.**

All persons, of whatever rank in the service, are required to observe respect toward sentinels and members of the guard when such are in the performance of their duties. (157)

A sentinel will at once report to the corporal of the guard every unusual or suspicious occurrence noted. (158)

He will arrest suspicious persons prowling about the post or camp at any time, all parties to a disorder occurring on or near his post, and all, except authorized persons, who attempt to enter the camp at night, and will turn over to the corporal of the guard all persons arrested. (159)

The number, limits, and extent of his post will invariably constitute part of the special orders of a sentinel on post. The limits of his post should be so defined as to include every place to which he is required to go in the performance of his duties. (160)

**No. 2: To walk my post in a military manner, keeping always on the alert and observing everything that takes place within sight or hearing.**

A sentinel is not required to halt and change the position of his rifle on arriving at the end of his post, nor to execute *to the rear, march,* precisely as prescribed in the drill regulations, but faces about while walking in the manner most convenient to him and at any part of his post as may be best suited to the proper performance of his duties. He carries his rifle on either shoulder, and in wet or severe weather, when not in a sentry box, may carry it at a secure. (161)

Sentinels when in sentry boxes stand at ease. Sentry boxes will be used in wet weather only, or at other times when specially authorized by the commanding officer. (162)

In very hot weather, sentinels may be authorized to stand at ease on their posts, provided they can effectively discharge their duties in this position; but they will take advantage of this privilege only on the express authority of the officer of the day or the commander of the guard. (163)

A mounted sentinel may dismount occasionally and lead his horse, but will not relax his vigilance. (164)

**No. 3: To report all violations of orders I am instructed to enforce.**

A sentinel will ordinarily report a violation of orders when he is inspected or relieved, but if the case be urgent, he will call the corporal of the guard, and also, if necessary, will arrest the offender. ·(165)

**No. 4: To repeat all calls from posts more distant from the guardhouse than my own.**

To call the corporal of the guard for any purpose other than relief, fire, or disorder (pars. 167 and 173), a sentinel will call "*Corporal of the guard, No.* (——)," adding the number of his post. In no case will any sentinel call, "*Never mind the corporal*"; nor will the corporal heed such call if given. (166)

**No. 5: To quit my post only when properly relieved.**

If relief becomes necessary, by reason of sickness or other cause, a sentinel will call, "*Corporal of the guard, No.* (——), *Relief,*" giving the number of his post. (167)

Whenever a sentinel is to be relieved, he will halt, and with arms at a right shoulder, will face toward the relief, when it is 30 paces from him. He will come to a port arms with the new sentinel, and in a low tone will transmit to him all the special orders relating to the post and any other information which will assist him to better perform his duties. (168)

**No. 6: To receive, obey, and pass on to the sentinel who relieves me, all orders from the commanding officer, officer of the day, and officers and noncommissioned officers of the guard only.**

During his tour of duty a soldier is subject to the orders of the commanding officer, officer of the day, and officers and noncommissioned officers of the guard only; but any officer is competent to investigate apparent violations of regulations of members of the guard. (169)

A sentinel will quit his piece on an explicit order from any person from whom he lawfully receives orders while on post; under no circumstances will he yield it to any other person. Unless necessity therefor exists, no person will require a sentinel to quit his piece, even to allow it to be inspected. (170)

A sentinel will not divulge the countersign (pars. 209 to 217) to anyone except the sentinel who relieves him, or to a person from whom he properly receives orders, on such persons verbal order given personally. Privates of the guard will not use the countersign except in the performance of their duties while posted as sentinels. (171)  •

## No. 7: To talk to no one except in line of duty.

When calling for any purpose, challenging, or holding communication with any person, a dismounted sentinel armed with a rifle or saber will take the position of port arms or saber. At night a dismounted sentinel armed with a pistol takes the position of raised pistol in challenging or holding communication. A mounted sentinel does not ordinarily draw his weapon in the daytime when challenging or holding conversation; but if drawn, he holds it at advance rifle, raise pistol, or port saber, according as he is armed with a rifle, pistol, or saber. At night in challenging and holding conversation his weapon is drawn and held as just prescribed, depending on whether he is armed with a rifle, pistol, or saber. (172)

## No. 8: In case of fire or disorder to give the alarm.

In case of fire, a sentinel will call, *"Fire, No. (——),"* adding the number of his post; if possible, he will extinguish the fire himself. In case of disorder he will call, *"The Guard, No. (——),"* adding the number of his post. If the danger be great, he will in either case discharge his piece before calling. (173)

## No. 11: To salute all officers and all colors and standards not cased.

When not engaged in the performance of a specific duty, the proper execution of which would prevent it, a member of the guard will salute all officers who pass him. This rule applies at all hours of the day or night, except is the case of mounted sentinels armed with a rifle or pistol, or dismounted sentinels armed with a pistol, after challenging. (See par. 181). (174)

Sentinels will salute as follows: A dismounted sentinel armed with a rifle or saber, salutes by presenting arms; if otherwise armed, he salutes with the right hand.

A mounted sentinel, if armed with a saber and the saber be drawn, salutes by presenting saber; otherwise he salutes in all cases with the right hand. (175)

To salute, a dismounted sentinel, with piece at a right shoulder or saber at a carry, halts and faces toward the person to be saluted when the latter arrives within 30 paces.

The limit within which indivduals and insignia of rank can be readily recognized is assumed to be about 30 paces, and therefore at this distance cognizance is taken of the person or party to be saluted. (176)

The salute is rendered at six paces; if the person to be saluted does not arrive within that distance, then when he is nearest. (177)

A sentinel in a sentry box, armed with a rifle, stands at attention in the doorway on the approach of a person or party entitled to salute, and salutes by presenting arms according to the foregoing rules.

If armed with a saber, he stands at a carry and salutes as before. (178)

A mounted sentinel on a regular post, halts, faces, and salutes in accordance with the foregoing rules. If doing patrol duty, he salutes, but does not halt unless spoken to. (179)

Sentinels salute, in accordance with the foregoing rules, all persons and parties entitled to compliments from the guards (pars. 224, 227, and 228); officers of the Army, Navy, and Marine Corps; military and naval officers of foreign powers; officers of volunteers and militia officers when in uniform. (180)

A sentinel salutes as just prescribed when an officer comes on his post; if the officer holds communication with the sentinel, the sentinel again salutes when the officer leaves him.

During the hours when challenging is prescribed, the first salute is given as soon as the officer has been duly recognized and advanced. A mounted sentinel armed with a rifle or pistol, or a dismounted sentinel armed with a pistol, does not salute after challenging.

He stands at advance rifle or raise pistol until the officer passes. (181)

In case of the approach of an armed party of the guard, the sentinel will halt when it is about 30 paces from him, facing toward the party with his piece at the right shoulder. If not himself relived , he will, as the party passes, place himself so that the party will pass in front of him; he resumes walking his post when the party has reached six paces beyond him. (182)

An officer is entitled to the compliments prescribed, whether in uniform or not. (183)

A sentinel in communication with an officer will not interrupt the conversation to salute. In the case of seniors the officer will salute, whereupon the sentinel will salute. (184)

When the flag is being lowered at retreat, a sentinel on post and in view of the flag will face the flag and, at the first note of the Star Spangled Banner or *to the color* will come to a present arms. At the sounding of the last note he will resume walking his post. (185)

**No. 12: To be especially watchful at night and during the time for challenging, to challenge all persons on or near my post, and to allow no one to pass without proper authority.**

During challenging hours, if a sentinel sees any person or party on or near his post, he will advance rapidly along his post toward such person or party and when within about 30 yards will challenge sharply, *"Halt, Who is there?"* He will place himself in the best possible position to receive or, if necessary, to arrest the person or party. (186)

In case a mounted party be challenged, the sentinel will call, *"Halt, Dismount. Who is there?"* (187)

The sentinel will permit only one of any party to approach him for the purpose of giving the countersign (pars. 209 to 217), or, if no countersign be used, of being duly recognized. When this is done the whole party is advanced, i. e., allowed to pass. (188)

In all cases the sentinel must satisfy himself beyond a reasonable doubt that the parties are what they represent themselves to be and have a right to pass. If he is not satisfied, he must cause them to stand and call the corporal of the guard. So, likewise, if he have no authority to pass persons with the countersign, or when the party has not the countersign, or gives an incorrect one. (189)

A sentinel will not permit any person to approach so close as to prevent the proper use of his own weapon before recognizing the person or receiving the countersign. (190)

When two or more persons approach in one party, the sentinel, on receiving an answer that indicates that some one in the party has the countersign, will say, *"Advance one with the countersign,"* and , if the countersign is given correctly, will then say,*"Advance (so and so),"* repeating the answer to his challenge. Thus if the answer be *"Relief (friend with the countersign, patrol, etc.),'* the sentinel will say, *"Advance one with the countersign;"* then *"Advance, relief (friends, patrol, etc.)."* (191)

If a person having the countersign approach alone, he is advanced to give the countersign. Thus if the answer be *"Friend with the countersign (or officer of the day, or etc.),"* the sentinel will say, *"Advance, friend (or officer of the day, or etc.) with the countersign;"* then *"Advance, friend (or officer of the day, or etc.)."* (192)

If two or more persons approach a sentinel's post from different directions at the same time, all such persons are challenged in turn and required to halt and to remain halted until advanced.

The senior is first advanced, in accordance with the foregoing rules. (193)

If a party is already advanced and in communication with a sentinel, the latter will challenge any other party that may approach; if the party challenged be senior to the one already on his post, the sentinel will advance the new party at once. The senior may allow him to advance any or all of the other parties; otherwise the sentinel will not advance any of them until the senior leaves him. He will then advance the senior only of the remaining parties, and so on. (194)

The following order of rank will govern a sentinel in advancing different persons or parties approaching his post: Commanding officers, officer of the day, officer of the guard, officers, patrols, reliefs, noncommissioned officers of the guard in order of rank, friends. (195)

A sentinel will never allow himself to be surprised, nor permit two parties to advance upon him at the same time. (196)

If no countersign be used, the rules for challenging are the same. The rules for advancing parties are modified only as follows: Instead of saying *"Advance (so-and-so) with the countersign,"* the sentinel will say, *"Advance (so-and-so) to be recognized."* Upon recognition he will say, *"Advance (so-and-so)."* (197)

Answers to a sentinel's challenge intended to confuse or mislead him are prohibited, but the use of such an answer as *"Friends with the countersign,"* is not to be understood as misleading, but as the usual answer made by officers, patrols, etc., when the purpose of their visit makes it desirable that their official capacity should not be announced.    (198)

## Special Orders for Sentinels at the Post of the Guard

Sentinels posted at the guard will be required to memorize the following:

*Between reveille and retreat to turn out the guard for all persons designated by the commanding officer, for all colors or standards not cased, and in time of war for all armed parties approaching my post, except troops at drill and reliefs and detachments of the guard.*

*At night, after challenging any person or party, to advance no one but call the corporal of the guard, repeating the answer to the challenge.*    (199)

After receiving an answer to his challenge, the sentinel calls, *"Corporal of the guard (so-and-so)*," repeating the answer to the challenge.    (200)

He does not in such cases repeat the number of his post.

He remains in the position assumed in challenging until the corporal has recognized or advanced the person or party challenged, when he resumes walking his post, or, if the person or party be entitled thereto, he salutes and, as soon as the salute has been acknowledged, resumes walking his post.    (201)

The sentinel at the post of the guard will be notified by direction of the commanding officer of the presence in camp or garrison of persons entitled to the compliment.    (Par. 224.) (202)

The following examples illustrate the manner in which the sentinel at the post of the guard will turn out the guard upon the approach of persons or parties entitled to the compliment (pars. 224, 227, and 228), *"Turn out the guard, commanding officer;" "Turn out the guard, governor of a Territory;" "Turn out the guard, national colors;" "Turn out the guard, armed party;"* etc.

At the approach of the new guard at guard mounting the sentinel will call, *"Turn out the guard, armed party."*    (203)

Should the person named by the sentinel not desire the guard formed, he will salute, whereupon the sentinel will call *"Never mind the guard."*    (204)

After having called *"Turn out the guard,"* the sentinel will never call *"Never mind the guard,"* on the approach of an armed party.    (205)

Though the guard be already formed he will not fail to call, *"Turn out the guard,"* as required in his special orders, except that the guard will not be turned out for any person while his senior is at or coming to the post of the guard. (206)

The sentinels at the post of the guard will warn the commander of the approach of any armed body and of the presence in the vicinity of all suspicious or disorderly persons. (207)

In case of fire or disorder in sight or hearing, the sentinel at the guardhouse will call the corporal of the guard and report the facts to him. (208)

## Countersigns and Paroles

The *parole* is a word used as a check on the countersign in order to obtain more accurate identification of persons. It is imparted only to those who are entitled to inspect guards and to commanders of guards. (211)

The parole or countersign, or both, are sent sealed in the form of an order to those entitled to them.

When the commander of the guard demands the parole, he will advance and receive it as the corporal receives the countersign. (See par. 133.) (212)

As the communications containing the parole and countersign must at times be distributed by many orderlies, the parole intrusted to many officers, and the countersign and parole to many officers and sentinels, and as both the countersign and parole must, for large commands, be prepared several days in advance, there is always danger of their being lost or becoming known to persons who would make improper use of them; moreover, a sentinel is too apt to take it for granted that any person who gives the right countersign is what he represents himself to be; hence for outpost duty there is a greater security in omitting the use of the countersign and parole, or in using them with great caution. The chief reliance should be upon personal recognition or identification of all persons claiming authority to pass.

Persons whose sole means of identification is the countersign, or concerning whose authority to pass there is a reasonable doubt, should not be allowed to pass without the authority of the corporal of the guard after proper investigation; the corporal will take to his next superior any person about whom he is not competent to decide. (213)

The *countersign* is usually the name of a battle; the *parole,* that of a general or other distinguished person. (214)

When they can not be communicated daily, a series of words for some days in advance may be sent to posts or detachments

that are to use the same parole or countersign as the main
body. (215)

If the countersign be lost, or if a member of the guard
deserts with it, the commander on the spot will substitute another for it and report the case at once to headquarters. (216)

In addition to the countersign, use may be made of precon-
certed signals, such as striking the rifle with the hand or
striking the hands together a certain number of times as agreed
upon. Such signals may be used only by guards that occupy
exposed points.

They are used before the countersign is given and must not
be communicated to anyone not entitled to know the countersign. Their use is intended to prevent the surprise of a
sentinel.

In the daytime signals such as raising a cap or a handker-
chief in a prearranged manner may be used by sentinels to
communicate with the guard or with each other. (217)

## Compliments from Guards

The compliment from a guard consists in the guard turning
out and presenting arms. (See par. 50.) No compliments
will be paid between retreat and reveille except as provided in
paragraphs 361 and 362, nor will any person other than those
named in paragraph 224 receive the compliment. (222)

Though a guard does not turn out between retreat and
reveille, as a matter of compliment it may be turned out for
inspection at any time by a person entitled to inspect it. (223)

Between reveille and retreat the following persons are entitled to the compliment: The President; sovereign or chief
magistrate of a foreign country and members of a royal family;
Vice President; President and President pro tempore of the
Senate; American and foreign ambassadors; members of the
Cabinet; Chief Justice; Speaker of the House of Representatives; committees of Congress officially visiting a military post;
governors within their respective States and Territories; governors general; Assistant Secretary of War officially visiting
a military post; all general officers of the Army; general
officers of foreign services visiting a post; naval, marine, volunteer, and militia officers in the service of the United States
and holding the rank of general officer; American or foreign
envoys or ministers; ministers accredited to the United States;
chargés d'affaires accredited to the United States; consuls
general accredited to the United States; commanding officer
of the post or camp; officer of the day. (224)

The relative rank between officers of the Army and Navy is as follows: General with admiral, lieutenant general with vice admiral, major general with rear admiral, brigadier general with commodore, colonel with captain, lieutenant colonel with commander, major with lieutenant commander, captain with lieutenant, first lieutenant with lieutenant (junior grade), second lieutenant with ensign. (A. R. 12.)  (225)

Sentinels will not be required to memorize paragraph 224, and, except in the cases of general officers of the Army, the commanding officer and the officer of the day will be advised in each case of the presence in camp or garrison of persons entitled to the compliment.  (226)

Guards will turn out and present arms when the national or regimental colors or standards, not cased, are carried past by a guard or an armed party. This rule also applies when the party carrying the colors is at drill. If the drill is conducted in the vicinity of the guardhouse, the guard will be turned out when the colors first pass and not thereafter.  (227)

In case the remains of a deceased officer or soldier are carried past, the guard will turn out and present arms.  (228)

In time of war all guards will turn out under arms when armed parties except troops at drill and reliefs or detachments of the guard approach their post. (See par. 53.)  (229)

## GENERAL RULES

The commander of the guard will be notified of the presence in camp or garrison of all persons entitled to the compliment except general officers of the Army, the commanding officer, and the officer of the day. Members of the guard will salute all persons entitled to the compliment and all officers in the military or naval service of foreign powers, officers of the Army, Navy and Marine Corps, officers of volunteers, and officers of militia when in uniform.  (230)

### General Rules Concerning Guard Duty

*Eighty-fifth article of war.*— * * * Any person subject to military law, except an officer, who is found drunk on duty shall be punished as a court-martial may direct.  (232)

All material instructions given to a member of the guard by an officer having authority will be promptly communicated to the commander of the guard by the officer giving them.  (233)

Should the guard be formed, soldiers will fall in ranks under arms. At roll call each man, as his name or number and relief are called, will answer "Here," and come to an *order arms.* (234)

Whenever the guard or a relief is dismissed, each member not at once required for duty will place his rifle in the arm racks, if they be provided, and will not remove it therefrom unless he requires it in the performance of some duty. (235)

Without permission from the commander of the guard, members of the main guard, except orderlies, will not leave the immediate vicinity of the guardhouse. Permission to leave will not be granted except in cases of necessity. (236)

Members of the main guard, except orderlies, will not remove their accouterments or clothing without permission from the commander of the guard. (Par. 66.) (237)

## Guarding Prisoners

The sentinel at the post of the guard has charge of the prisoners except when they have been turned over to the prisoner guard or overseers. (Pars. 247 and 300 to 304.)

(a) He will allow none to escape.

(b) He will allow none to cross his post leaving the guardhouse except when passed by an officer or noncommissioned officer of the guard.

(c) He will allow no one to communicate with prisoners without permission from proper authority.

(d) He will promptly report to the corporal of the guard any suspicious noise made by the prisoners.

(e) He will be prepared to tell whenever asked, how many prisoners are in the guardhouse and how many are out at work or elsewhere.

Whenever prisoners are brought to his post returning from work or elsewhere, he will halt them and call the corporal of the guard, notifying him of the number of prisoners returning. Thus: *"Corporal of the guard, (so many) prisoners."*

He will not allow prisoners to pass into the guardhouse until the corporal of the guard has responded to the call and ordered him to do so. (299)

Whenever practicable, special guards will be detailed for the particular duty of guarding working parties composed of such prisoners as can not be placed under overseers. (Par. 247.) (300)

The prisoner guard and overseers will be commanded by the police officer; if there be no police officer, then by the officer of the day. (301)

Details for prisoner guard are marched to the guardhouse and mounted by being inspected by the commander of the main guard, who determines whether all of the men are in proper condition to perform their duties and whether their arms and equipments are in proper condition, and rejects any men found unfit. (303)

When prisoners have been turned over to the prisoner guard or overseers, such guards or overseers are responsible for them under their commander, and all responsibility and control of the main guard ceases until they are returned to the main guard. (Par. 306.) (304)

If a prisoner attempts to escape, the sentinel will call *"Halt."* If he fails to halt when the sentinel has once repeated his call, and if there be no other possible means of preventing his escape, the sentinel will fire upon him.

The following will more fully explain the important duties of a sentinel in this connection:

(Circular.)  WAR DEPARTMENT,
ADJUTANT GENERAL'S OFFICE,
*Washington, November* 1, 1887.

By direction of the Secretary of War, the following is published for the information of the Army:

UNITED STATES CIRCUIT COURT, EASTERN DISTRICT OF MICHIGAN, AUGUST 1, 1887.
THE UNITED STATES V. JAMES CLARK.

The circuit court has jurisdiction of a homicide committed by one soldier upon another within a military reservation of the United States.

If a homicide be committed by a military guard without malice and in the performance of his supposed duty as a soldier, such homicide is excusable, unless it was manifestly beyond the scope of his authority or was such that a man of ordinary sense and understanding would know that it was illegal.

It seems that the sergeant of the guard has a right to shoot a military convict if there be no other possible means of preventing his escape.

The common-law distinction between felonies and misdemeanors has no application to military offenses.

While the finding of a court of inquiry acquitting the prisoner of all blame is not a legal bar to a prosecution, it is entitled to weight as an expression of the views of the military court of the necessity of using a musket to prevent the escape of the deceased.

\*    \*    \*    \*    \*    \*    \*

By order of the Secretary of War:
R. C. DRUM, *Adjutant General.*

The following is taken from Circular No. 3, of 1883, from Headquarters Department of the Columbia:

VANCOUVER BARRACKS, W. T., *April 20, 1883.*
To the ASSISTANT ADJUTANT GENERAL,
*Department of the Columbia.*

SIR:

\*　　\*　　\*　　\*　　\*　　\*　　\*

A sentinel is placed as guard over prisoners to prevent their escape, and, for this purpose, he is furnished a musket, with ammunition. To prevent escape is his first and most important duty.

\*　　\*　　\*　　\*　　\*　　\*　　\*

I suppose the law to be this: That a sentinel shall not use more force or violence to prevent the escape of a prisoner than is necessary to effect that object, but if the prisoner, after being ordered to halt, continues his flight, the sentinel may maim or even kill him, and it is his duty to do so.

A sentinel who allows a prisoner to escape without firing upon him, and firing to hit him, is in my judgment, guilty of a most serious military offense, for which he should and would be severely punished by a general court-martial.

\*　　\*　　\*　　\*　　\*　　\*　　\*

(Signed)　　HENRY A. MORROW,
*Colonel Twenty-first Infantry, Commanding Post.*

[Third indorsement.]

OFFICE JUDGE ADVOCATE,
MILITARY DIVISION OF THE PACIFIC,
*May 11, 1883.*

Respectfully returned to the assistant adjutant general, Military Division of the Pacific, concurring fully in the views expressed by Col. Morrow. I was not aware that such a view had ever been questioned. That the period is a time of peace does not affect the authority and duty of the sentinel or guard to fire upon the escaping prisoner, if this escape can not otherwise be prevented. He should, of course, attempt to stop the prisoner before firing by ordering him to halt, and will properly warn him by the words "Halt, or I fire," or words to such effect.

W. WINTHROP, *Judge Advocate.*

[Fourth indorsement.]

HEADQUARTERS MILITARY DIVISION OF THE PACIFIC,
*May* 11, 1883.

Respectfully returned to the commanding general, Department of the Columbia, approving the opinion of the commanding officer, Twenty-first Infantry, and of the judge advocate of the division, in respect to the duty and method to be adopted adopted by sentinels in preventing prisoners from escaping.

\*     \*     \*     \*     \*     \*     \*

By command of Maj. Gen. Schofield:

J. C. KELTON,
*Assistant Adjutant General.*

See also Circular No. 53, A. G. O., December 22, 1900. (305)

On approaching the post of the sentinel at the guardhouse, a sentinel of the prisoner guard or an overseer in charge of prisoners will halt them and call, *"No.* 1 (*so many*) *prisoners."* He will not allow them to cross the post of the sentinel until so directed by the corporal of the guard.

Members of the prisoner guard and overseers placed over prisoners for work will receive specific and explicit instructions covering the required work; they will be held strictly responsible that the prisoners under their charge properly and satisfactorily perform the designated work. (307)

### Flags

At every military post or station the flag will be hoisted at the sounding of the first note of the reveille, or of the first note of the march, if a march be played before the reveille. The flag will be lowered at the sounding of the last note of the retreat, and while the flag is being lowered the band will play "The Star-Spangled Banner," or, if there be no band present, the field music will sound "to the color." When "to the color" is sounded by the field music while the flag is being lowered the same respect will be observed as when "The Star-Spangled Banner" is played by the band, and in either case officers and enlisted men out of ranks will face toward the flag, stand at attention, and render the prescribed salute at the last note of the music. (A. R. 437.)

The lowering of the flag will be so regulated as to be completed at the last note of "The Star-Spangled Banner" or "to the color." (338)

The national flag will be displayed at a seacoast or lake fort at the beginning of and during an action in which a fort may be enegaged, whether by day or by night. (A. R. 437.) (339)

The national flag will always be displayed at the time of firing a salute. (A. R. 397.) (340)

The flag of a military post will not be dipped by way of salute or compliment. (A. R. 405.) (341)

On the death of an officer at a military post the flag is displayed at halfstaff and so remains between reveille and retreat until the last salvo or volley is fired over the grave; or if the remains are not interred at the post until they are removed therefrom. (A. R. 422.) (342)

During the funeral of an enlisted man at a military post the flag is displayed at halfstaff. It is hoisted to the top after the final volley or gun is fired or after the remains are taken from the post. The same honors are paid on the occasion of the funeral of a retired enlisted man. (A. R. 423.) (343)

When practicable, a detail consisting of a noncommissioned officer and two privates of the guard will raise or lower the flag. This detail wears side arms or if the special equipments do not include side arms then belts only.

The noncommissioned officer, carrying the flag, forms the detail in line, takes his post in the center and marches it to the staff. The flag is then securely attached to the halyards and rapidly hoisted. The halyards are then securely fastened to the cleat on the staff and the detail marched to the guardhouse. (344)

When the flag is to be lowered, the halyards are loosened from the staff and made perfectly free. At retreat the flag is lowered at the last note of retreat. It is then neatly folded and the halyards made fast. The detail is then re-formed and marched to the guardhouse, where the flag is turned over to the commander of the guard.

The flag should never be allowed to touch the ground and should always be hoisted or lowered from the leeward side of the staff, the halyards being held by two persons. (345)

## Reveille and Retreat Gun

The morning and evening gun will be fired by a detachment of the guard, consisting, when practicable, of a corporal and two privates. The morning gun is fired at the first note of reveille, or, if marches be played before the reveille, it is fired at the beginning of the first march. The retreat gun is fired at the last note of retreat.

The corporal marches the detachment to and from the piece, which is fired, sponged out, and secured under his direction. (346)

# INDEX

# INDEX